THE
DARK
TRIAD

Deep Delve into Twisted Minds

Published By: Pierre G. Valen

THANK YOU!

Thank you for purchasing my book. Your support means the world to me, and I truly hope you found value in these pages. If you enjoyed the content and it helped you in any way, I would greatly appreciate it if you could take a moment to leave a positive review on Amazon. Your feedback not only helps others discover the book but also encourages me to keep creating content that adds value to readers like you.

Once again, thank you for your trust and support. It wouldn't be possible without readers like you!

TABLE OF CONTENTS

Introduction

In the realm of psychology, few concepts have captured the imagination and concern of both professionals and the general public quite like the Dark Triad. This psychological construct, comprising three distinct yet interrelated personality traits - narcissism, Machiavellianism, and psychopathy - has become a focal point for understanding some of the most complex and potentially dangerous individuals in our society. These traits, when found in combination, often result in a personality profile that is manipulative, self-serving, and capable of inflicting significant harm on others without remorse.

Narcissism, the first component of the Dark Triad, is characterized by an inflated sense of self-importance, a deep-seated need for excessive attention and admiration, and a lack of empathy for others. Individuals high in narcissism often exhibit grandiose behaviors, believing themselves to be superior to those around them and deserving of special treatment. This trait can manifest in various ways, from the seemingly harmless pursuit of social media fame to the more sinister exploitation of others for personal gain.

Machiavellianism, named after the Italian Renaissance diplomat Niccolò Machiavelli, refers to a personality trait marked by cunning, manipulation, and a willingness to deceive others to achieve one's goals. Those high in Machiavellianism tend to be strategic thinkers, adept at reading and exploiting the weaknesses of others. They often possess a cynical worldview and a pragmatic approach to morality, viewing ethical considerations as secondary to their personal objectives.

Psychopathy, perhaps the most chilling of the three traits, is characterized by a lack of empathy, impulsivity, and a tendency towards antisocial behavior. Psychopaths often display superficial charm and charisma, using these qualities to mask their true nature and manipulate others. They may engage in risky or criminal behavior without regard for consequences, showing little remorse for the harm they cause to others.

While these traits can exist independently, their combination in the Dark Triad creates a particularly potent and potentially dangerous personality profile. Individuals who score high on all three traits often possess a unique ability to navigate social situations to their advantage, leaving a trail of manipulation and exploitation in their wake. The Dark Triad has become a subject of intense study and fascination, not only for its implications in clinical psychology but also for its relevance in various aspects of society, from business and politics to interpersonal relationships.

Throughout history, the traits associated with the Dark Triad have played significant roles in shaping events and influencing the course of human civilization. From ancient tyrants who ruled through fear and manipulation to modern-day corporate leaders who prioritize profit over ethics, the impact of these personality traits has been profound and far-reaching. In the annals of history, we find numerous examples of individuals who have exhibited these characteristics, often rising to positions of power and influence through their ability to manipulate and exploit others.

In today's society, the relevance of the Dark Triad has only grown more pronounced. The rise of social media and the increasing importance of personal branding have created new avenues for narcissistic individuals to seek attention and admiration. The competitive nature of the business world has, in some cases, rewarded Machiavellian tactics and a willingness to prioritize personal gain over ethical considerations. Meanwhile, the complex web of modern society has provided new opportunities for those with psychopathic tendencies to exploit vulnerabilities and evade consequences for their actions.

The prevalence of Dark Triad traits in positions of power and influence has raised important questions about the nature of leadership and success in our society. While these traits can sometimes contribute to short-term success, their long-term impact on organizations, communities, and individuals is often destructive. Understanding the Dark Triad has become crucial not only for mental health professionals but also for anyone seeking to navigate the complex social landscape of the modern world.

This book, "The Dark Triad: Deep Delve into Twisted Minds," aims to provide a comprehensive exploration of this fascinating and troubling psychological construct. By delving deep into the minds of those possessing these traits, we seek to unravel the complex interplay of factors that contribute to the development and expression of Dark Triad personalities. Through a careful dissection of each element of the triad - narcissism, Machiavellianism, and psychopathy - we will examine the underlying psychological mechanisms that drive these behaviors.

Our journey will take us beyond mere theoretical constructs, venturing into the realm of real-world examples that illustrate the impact of Dark Triad personalities in various contexts. From the boardrooms of major corporations to the intimate sphere of personal relationships, we will explore how these traits manifest in everyday life and the consequences they can have on individuals and society as a whole.

By examining case studies, analyzing research findings, and drawing insights from experts in the field, this book aims to provide readers with a nuanced understanding of the Dark Triad. We will explore the factors that contribute to the development of these traits, including genetic predispositions, environmental influences, and societal factors that may inadvertently reward or encourage such behaviors.

Moreover, we will delve into the ethical implications of studying and understanding the Dark Triad. As we gain greater insight into these personality traits, we must grapple with complex questions about free will, moral responsibility, and the potential for change or rehabilitation in individuals who exhibit these characteristics.

Throughout this exploration, we will also consider the implications of the Dark Triad for society at large. How do we protect ourselves and our institutions from the potentially destructive influence of individuals with these traits? What strategies can be employed to identify and mitigate the impact of Dark Triad personalities in various contexts, from personal relationships to professional environments?

By providing a comprehensive and accessible examination of the Dark Triad, this book seeks to empower readers with knowledge and understanding. Whether you are a mental health professional, a business leader, or simply someone interested in understanding human behavior, the insights contained within these pages will offer valuable perspectives on one of the most intriguing and concerning aspects of human psychology.

As we embark on this journey into the depths of the Dark Triad, we invite readers to approach the subject with an open mind and a critical eye. The exploration of these twisted minds offers not only a fascinating glimpse into the darker aspects of human nature but also an opportunity for self-reflection and growth. By understanding the mechanisms behind these traits, we can better equip ourselves to recognize and respond to them in our own lives and in the world around us.

Chapter 1: Meet The Narcissist

What is Narcissism?

Narcissism, from a psychological perspective, is a complex personality trait characterized by an inflated sense of self-importance, an excessive need for admiration, and a profound lack of empathy for others. This term, derived from the Greek myth of Narcissus, who fell in love with his own reflection, has evolved to describe a spectrum of behaviors and attitudes that revolve around self-aggrandizement and an insatiable hunger for attention and praise.

At its core, narcissism is rooted in a deep-seated insecurity and fragile self-esteem, masked by an outward display of confidence and superiority. Individuals with narcissistic traits often exhibit a grandiose sense of self-importance, believing they are special, unique, and deserving of constant admiration and special treatment. This inflated self-image is not grounded in reality but serves as a defense mechanism against feelings of inadequacy and vulnerability.

One of the primary characteristics of narcissism is grandiosity. Narcissists tend to exaggerate their achievements and talents, often portraying themselves as exceptionally gifted, successful, or powerful. They may engage in elaborate fantasies of unlimited success, power, brilliance, beauty, or ideal love. This grandiose behavior is not merely a display of confidence but an essential component of their identity, serving to reinforce their perceived superiority over others.

Entitlement is another hallmark of narcissistic behavior. Narcissists believe they deserve special privileges and treatment, regardless of their actual accomplishments or contributions. They expect unwavering compliance with their wishes and desires, often becoming enraged or deeply wounded when their expectations are not met. This sense of entitlement can manifest in various ways, from demanding preferential treatment in social situations to expecting others to cater to their every whim in personal relationships.

Perhaps one of the most damaging aspects of narcissism is the profound lack of empathy exhibited by those who possess this trait. Narcissists struggle to recognize or identify with the feelings and needs of others. They view people as extensions of themselves or as objects to be manipulated for their own gain. This inability to empathize makes it challenging for narcissists to form genuine, meaningful relationships, as they are primarily focused on how others can serve their needs and bolster their self-image.

The origins of narcissism are complex and multifaceted, with both genetic and environmental factors playing a role. Some researchers suggest that narcissistic traits may develop as a coping mechanism in response to childhood experiences of neglect, abuse, or excessive praise and indulgence. Others point to cultural factors, such as the rise of individualism and the emphasis on self-promotion in modern society, as contributing to the prevalence of narcissistic traits.

It's important to note that narcissism exists on a spectrum, ranging from healthy self-esteem to pathological narcissism. While some degree of self-love and confidence is necessary for psychological well-being, extreme narcissism can be debilitating for both the individual and those around them. At its most severe, narcissism may manifest as Narcissistic Personality Disorder (NPD), a clinical diagnosis characterized by a pervasive pattern of grandiosity, need for admiration, and lack of empathy.

Individuals with narcissistic traits often display a preoccupation with fantasies of unlimited success, power, brilliance, beauty, or ideal love. They believe they are "special" and can only be understood by, or should associate with, other special or high-status people or institutions. This belief in their own exceptionalism often leads them to seek out positions of power or influence, where they can receive the admiration and recognition they crave.

The narcissist's need for admiration is insatiable. They require constant attention and praise from others to maintain their inflated self-image. This can manifest in various ways, from dominating conversations to engaging in attention-seeking behaviors. Narcissists may become easily jealous or envious of others, particularly those who they perceive as threatening their status or receiving attention they believe should be directed towards them.

In interpersonal relationships, narcissists often exploit others for their own gain. They may use charm and charisma to initially attract people, but as relationships progress, their true nature becomes apparent. Narcissists typically lack the ability to form deep, meaningful connections with others, as they view relationships primarily as a means to fulfill their own needs and desires. They may engage in manipulative behaviors, such as gaslighting or emotional blackmail, to maintain control over others and preserve their own sense of superiority.

The narcissist's lack of empathy can have devastating effects on those close to them. They struggle to recognize or validate the emotions of others, often dismissing or minimizing the feelings and experiences of those around them. This emotional blindness can lead to a pattern of toxic relationships, where the narcissist's partners, friends, or family members feel consistently undervalued, misunderstood, and emotionally drained.

It's crucial to understand that narcissism, particularly in its more extreme forms, can have significant negative impacts on various aspects of an individual's life. In professional settings, narcissists may struggle with teamwork and collaboration, as they often believe their ideas and contributions are superior to those of their colleagues. Their inability to accept criticism or feedback can hinder personal growth and professional development.

In personal relationships, narcissists may experience a pattern of unstable and unfulfilling connections. Their constant need for admiration and lack of empathy can lead to conflicts, emotional abuse, and the eventual breakdown of relationships. Many narcissists find themselves in a cycle of idealization and devaluation, where they initially put their partners on a pedestal, only to become disillusioned and critical when their unrealistic expectations are not met.

The internal experience of a narcissist is often marked by a constant struggle to maintain their inflated self-image. Despite their outward appearance of confidence and self-assurance, many narcissists suffer from deep-seated insecurities and a fragile sense of self-worth. This internal conflict can lead to mood swings, irritability, and a persistent sense of emptiness or dissatisfaction.

Recognizing and understanding narcissism is crucial for both individuals who may exhibit narcissistic traits and those who interact with them. For those with narcissistic tendencies, acknowledging these patterns can be the first step towards developing healthier relationships and a more realistic self-image. For others, understanding the nature of narcissism can help in setting boundaries, protecting oneself from manipulation, and fostering more balanced and fulfilling relationships.

Types of Narcissism

Narcissism, like many psychological traits, exists on a spectrum and manifests in various forms. Understanding the different types of narcissism is crucial for recognizing and dealing with narcissistic individuals in both personal and professional settings. This section will explore the distinctions between overt and covert narcissism, as well as delve into the vulnerable and grandiose subtypes.

Overt narcissism is the more commonly recognized form of narcissistic behavior. Individuals exhibiting overt narcissism are often described as loud, attention-seeking, and overtly self-aggrandizing. They tend to dominate conversations, boast about their achievements, and demand admiration from others. Overt narcissists are typically extroverted and charismatic, using their charm to manipulate and control those around them. They have an inflated sense of self-importance and believe they are superior to others in every aspect of life.

These individuals often display a grandiose demeanor, expecting special treatment and privileges without necessarily having earned them. They may become easily offended or angered when their perceived superiority is challenged or when they don't receive the admiration they believe they deserve. Overt narcissists are more likely to engage in obvious self-promotion, such as constantly posting on social media about their accomplishments or surrounding themselves with status symbols.

In contrast, covert narcissism is a more subtle and less obvious form of narcissistic behavior. Covert narcissists share the same core beliefs of superiority and entitlement as their overt counterparts, but they express these traits in a more understated manner. These individuals often appear shy, introverted, or even self-deprecating on the surface. However, beneath this facade lies a deep-seated sense of grandiosity and a constant need for admiration.

Covert narcissists may engage in passive-aggressive behavior, subtle manipulation, and victimhood to gain attention and sympathy from others. They often harbor feelings of envy and resentment towards those they perceive as more successful or popular. Unlike overt narcissists who openly seek the spotlight, covert narcissists may fantasize about recognition and success while outwardly appearing modest or self-effacing.

These individuals may use their perceived victimhood as a tool to garner attention and manipulate others. They might frequently complain about being misunderstood or unappreciated, all while maintaining an air of superiority. Covert narcissists are often skilled at playing the "martyr" role, presenting themselves as selfless and long-suffering while secretly believing they are better than everyone else.

Within the broader categories of overt and covert narcissism, researchers have identified two primary subtypes: grandiose narcissism and vulnerable narcissism. These subtypes can manifest in both overt and covert forms, creating a complex tapestry of narcissistic behaviors and traits.

Grandiose narcissism is characterized by an exaggerated sense of self-importance, a preoccupation with fantasies of unlimited success and power, and a belief in one's own uniqueness and superiority. Individuals exhibiting grandiose narcissism often display a sense of entitlement, expecting others to cater to their needs and desires without reciprocation. They may exploit others for personal gain and show little empathy for those around them.

Grandiose narcissists are often charismatic and socially adept, using their charm to manipulate and influence others. They thrive on admiration and attention, constantly seeking validation from those around them. These individuals may engage in risky or impulsive behaviors to maintain their inflated self-image and prove their superiority to others.

In professional settings, grandiose narcissists may rise to positions of power due to their confidence and ability to self-promote. However, their leadership style is often characterized by a lack of empathy, an inability to accept criticism, and a tendency to take credit for others' work while blaming subordinates for failures.

Vulnerable narcissism, on the other hand, is marked by a more fragile and insecure sense of self. While vulnerable narcissists still harbor beliefs of superiority and entitlement, these beliefs are often accompanied by feelings of inadequacy, shame, and anxiety. These individuals are hypersensitive to criticism and may react with rage or withdrawal when their self-esteem is threatened.

Vulnerable narcissists often struggle with low self-esteem and may experience frequent mood swings. They may alternate between grandiose fantasies of success and periods of self-doubt and depression. Unlike grandiose narcissists who actively seek admiration, vulnerable narcissists may avoid social situations out of fear of rejection or criticism.

These individuals may engage in self-handicapping behaviors, sabotaging their own success to protect their fragile self-esteem. By creating excuses for their failures, they can maintain their belief in their own superiority while avoiding situations that might expose their perceived inadequacies.

In relationships, vulnerable narcissists may be clingy and demanding, constantly seeking reassurance and validation from their partners. They may become jealous easily and struggle with feelings of abandonment. Their relationships are often tumultuous, marked by periods of idealization followed by devaluation when their partner fails to meet their unrealistic expectations.

It's important to note that while these categories and subtypes provide a framework for understanding narcissistic behavior, individuals may exhibit traits from multiple categories. Narcissism is a complex personality trait that exists on a spectrum, and people may display different types of narcissistic behaviors depending on the situation and their emotional state.

Understanding the different types of narcissism can be valuable in various contexts. In clinical settings, it can help mental health professionals develop more targeted treatment approaches for individuals with narcissistic personality disorder. In personal relationships, recognizing the signs of different types of narcissism can help individuals set appropriate boundaries and protect themselves from manipulation and emotional abuse.

In the workplace, awareness of these different manifestations of narcissism can aid in identifying potentially problematic behaviors in colleagues or superiors. It can also inform hiring decisions and leadership development programs, helping organizations create healthier work environments and more effective teams.

As we continue to explore the complexities of narcissistic behavior throughout this book, it's crucial to remember that these categories are not rigid or all-encompassing. Each individual with narcissistic traits is unique, and their behavior may not fit neatly into any one category. By developing a nuanced understanding of the various types and subtypes of narcissism, we can better navigate our interactions with narcissistic individuals and develop more effective strategies for dealing with the challenges they present.

The Development of Narcissism

The development of narcissism is a complex process that begins in early childhood and continues to evolve throughout an individual's life. While some researchers argue for a genetic predisposition to narcissistic traits, the majority of evidence points to environmental factors as the primary contributors to the formation of narcissistic personalities. Understanding the origins of narcissism requires a deep dive into the intricate interplay between a child's innate temperament and the various external influences that shape their developing psyche.

The foundations of narcissism are often laid in the earliest years of life, during the critical period of attachment formation between a child and their primary caregivers. Attachment theory, pioneered by John Bowlby, suggests that the quality of these early relationships profoundly impacts a child's emotional development and future interpersonal relationships. In the case of narcissism, two seemingly contradictory parenting styles have been identified as potential catalysts: excessive indulgence and severe neglect or abuse.

Overly indulgent parenting, characterized by constant praise, lack of boundaries, and an emphasis on the child's specialness, can foster an inflated sense of self-importance. Children raised in such environments may develop an expectation of continued admiration and special treatment from others, leading to the grandiose self-image typical of narcissistic individuals. These children often struggle to develop a realistic self-concept, as their accomplishments and abilities are consistently overvalued by their caregivers.

Conversely, severe neglect or abuse can also contribute to the development of narcissistic traits. In these cases, children may construct a grandiose self-image as a defense mechanism against feelings of worthlessness and inadequacy. By creating an idealized version of themselves, they attempt to compensate for the lack of love, attention, or validation they experienced in their formative years. This defensive narcissism serves as a psychological shield, protecting the individual from confronting their deep-seated insecurities and unmet emotional needs.

The role of parental narcissism cannot be overlooked in the development of narcissistic traits in children. Narcissistic parents often view their children as extensions of themselves, using them to fulfill their own needs for admiration and achievement. These parents may alternately idealize and devalue their children, creating an unstable emotional environment that hampers the development of a healthy self-concept. Children of narcissistic parents may internalize these patterns, either by emulating their parents' narcissistic behaviors or by developing narcissistic traits as a means of coping with their unpredictable upbringing.

Sibling relationships and birth order can also play a significant role in the development of narcissism. First-born or only children may be more susceptible to developing narcissistic traits due to the increased attention and expectations placed upon them by their parents. Similarly, children who are consistently favored over their siblings may develop an inflated sense of self-importance, while those who are routinely compared unfavorably to their siblings may develop narcissistic traits as a compensatory mechanism.

The broader cultural context in which a child grows up can significantly influence the development of narcissistic traits. Western societies, particularly in the United States, have been criticized for promoting individualism and self-promotion to an extent that may foster narcissistic tendencies. The rise of social media and the constant pursuit of likes, followers, and online validation has created an environment where self-aggrandizement is not only accepted but often rewarded. Children and adolescents growing up in this digital age may be particularly vulnerable to developing narcissistic traits as they navigate the complex world of online identity and self-presentation.

Educational environments can also contribute to the development of narcissism. Educational systems that prioritize individual achievement and competition over cooperation and empathy may inadvertently reinforce narcissistic tendencies. The pressure to stand out and excel can lead some students to develop an inflated sense of their abilities and a diminished capacity for recognizing the achievements of others. Additionally, educational practices that emphasize self-esteem building without a corresponding emphasis on empathy and social responsibility may unintentionally promote narcissistic traits.

Peer relationships during childhood and adolescence play a crucial role in shaping personality traits, including narcissism. Children who consistently receive admiration and special treatment from their peers may develop an expectation for continued adulation, reinforcing narcissistic tendencies. Conversely, those who experience rejection or bullying may develop narcissistic traits as a defense mechanism, creating a grandiose self-image to protect against feelings of inadequacy and social exclusion.

Traumatic experiences during childhood or adolescence can also contribute to the development of narcissistic traits. Severe trauma, such as physical or sexual abuse, can disrupt normal personality development and lead to the formation of maladaptive coping mechanisms. In some cases, individuals may develop narcissistic traits as a way of regaining a sense of control and power in the aftermath of traumatic experiences.

The development of narcissism is not a fixed process that ends in childhood or adolescence. Throughout adulthood, various life experiences and environmental factors can either reinforce or mitigate narcissistic traits. Professional success, particularly in fields that offer high levels of public recognition or financial reward, can fuel narcissistic tendencies in individuals who are already predisposed to such traits. Conversely, experiences of failure, rejection, or loss may challenge narcissistic defenses and potentially lead to a re-evaluation of one's self-concept.

Romantic relationships can also play a significant role in the reinforcement or moderation of narcissistic traits. Individuals with narcissistic tendencies may seek out partners who provide constant admiration and validation, further entrenching their grandiose self-image. However, healthy relationships that provide honest feedback and encourage personal growth may help to temper narcissistic traits over time.

It is important to note that while certain environmental factors and experiences may increase the likelihood of developing narcissistic traits, not all individuals exposed to these influences will become narcissists. The development of narcissism is a complex interplay between genetic predisposition, early childhood experiences, and ongoing environmental factors. Some individuals may possess protective factors, such as resilience or strong support systems, that mitigate the impact of potentially narcissism-inducing experiences.

Understanding the multifaceted origins of narcissism is crucial for developing effective prevention and intervention strategies. By addressing the root causes of narcissistic traits in childhood and creating environments that foster empathy, realistic self-appraisal, and healthy interpersonal relationships, we may be able to reduce the prevalence of pathological narcissism in society. Moreover, this knowledge can inform therapeutic approaches for individuals struggling with narcissistic traits, helping them to develop more adaptive ways of relating to themselves and others.

Narcissism in Popular Culture

The portrayal of narcissists in popular culture has become increasingly prevalent in recent years, reflecting a growing societal awareness and fascination with this personality trait. From literature to film, television to social media, narcissistic characters have captured the imagination of audiences worldwide. These representations not only mirror existing perceptions of narcissism but also play a significant role in shaping public understanding and attitudes towards narcissistic individuals.

In literature, narcissistic characters have long been a staple of storytelling. Classic works such as Oscar Wilde's "The Picture of Dorian Gray" and F. Scott Fitzgerald's "The Great Gatsby" feature protagonists with distinct narcissistic traits. Dorian Gray's obsession with his own beauty and youth, and Jay Gatsby's grandiose self-image and relentless pursuit of status, exemplify different facets of narcissism. These early portrayals often focused on the tragic consequences of unchecked self-absorption, serving as cautionary tales about the dangers of excessive self-love.

Modern literature has continued to explore narcissism, often with more nuanced and psychologically informed depictions. Novels like Bret Easton Ellis's "American Psycho" and Gillian Flynn's "Gone Girl" present complex narcissistic characters whose actions blur the lines between reality and delusion. These works delve deeper into the inner workings of narcissistic minds, offering readers a chilling glimpse into the thought processes and motivations that drive such individuals.

In cinema, narcissistic characters have evolved from being mere antagonists to becoming central figures in their own right. Films like "The Wolf of Wall Street" and "There Will Be Blood" showcase charismatic yet deeply flawed protagonists whose narcissism fuels their ambition and eventual downfall. These portrayals often walk a fine line between condemnation and admiration, reflecting society's conflicted attitudes towards successful yet morally questionable individuals.

Television has provided a particularly fertile ground for exploring narcissism, with long-form storytelling allowing for more in-depth character development. Series like "Mad Men" and "Succession" feature ensemble casts populated by narcissistic characters, each exhibiting different manifestations of the trait. These shows often examine how narcissism intersects with power, ambition, and family dynamics, offering a more nuanced view of how narcissistic tendencies play out in various contexts.

Reality television has also contributed significantly to the cultural discourse on narcissism. Shows like "Keeping Up with the Kardashians" and various competition-based programs often showcase individuals with apparent narcissistic traits. While these portrayals are often exaggerated for entertainment value, they have undoubtedly influenced public perceptions of narcissism, sometimes blurring the line between healthy self-confidence and pathological self-absorption.

Social media platforms have emerged as a new frontier for the exploration and expression of narcissistic tendencies. The rise of influencer culture and the emphasis on personal branding have created an environment where narcissistic behaviors are often rewarded with attention and financial success. This has led to a complex interplay between media representations and real-world behavior, with some arguing that social media actively encourages and amplifies narcissistic traits.

The portrayal of narcissists in popular culture has had a significant impact on societal perceptions of the trait. On one hand, these representations have increased public awareness of narcissism as a psychological concept, helping people recognize and understand narcissistic behaviors in their own lives. This heightened awareness has contributed to more open discussions about mental health and personality disorders, potentially reducing stigma and encouraging those affected to seek help.

However, the prevalence of narcissistic characters in media has also led to some misconceptions and oversimplifications. The term "narcissist" is often used casually to describe anyone exhibiting self-centered behavior, potentially trivializing the clinical definition of Narcissistic Personality Disorder. Additionally, the frequent portrayal of narcissists as charismatic and successful individuals may inadvertently glamorize narcissistic traits, leading some to view them as desirable or necessary for achievement.

The influence of these portrayals extends beyond individual perceptions to broader cultural trends. Some scholars argue that the increased visibility of narcissistic characters in media reflects and reinforces a cultural shift towards individualism and self-promotion. This has sparked debates about whether society is becoming more narcissistic as a whole, or if media representations are simply making existing narcissistic tendencies more apparent.

It's important to note that while media portrayals of narcissism can be informative and thought-provoking, they should not be considered substitutes for clinical diagnosis or professional understanding of Narcissistic Personality Disorder. Many fictional depictions of narcissists focus on the more dramatic or extreme manifestations of the trait, potentially overlooking the subtler and more common expressions of narcissism in everyday life.

The entertainment industry's approach to narcissism has also evolved over time, reflecting changing societal attitudes and increased psychological understanding. While earlier portrayals often painted narcissists as one-dimensional villains or comic relief, contemporary representations tend to offer more complex and humanizing depictions. This shift allows audiences to engage with narcissistic characters on a deeper level, exploring the underlying insecurities and traumas that often contribute to narcissistic behavior.

As public interest in narcissism continues to grow, it's likely that media representations will continue to evolve and diversify. Future portrayals may focus more on the impact of narcissism on relationships and communities, or explore the intersection of narcissism with other personality traits and disorders. There may also be increased attention to cultural differences in the expression and perception of narcissistic traits, moving beyond the predominantly Western perspective that has dominated media representations thus far.

The portrayal of narcissists in popular culture serves as both a mirror and a shaping force for societal understanding of this complex personality trait. While these representations have undoubtedly increased public awareness and sparked important conversations, they also carry the potential for oversimplification and misunderstanding. As consumers of media, it's crucial to approach these portrayals with a critical eye, recognizing their value in stimulating discussion while also acknowledging their limitations as artistic interpretations rather than clinical realities.

Chapter 2: Machiavellianism Unveiled

What is Machiavellianism?

Machiavellianism is a personality trait characterized by cunning, manipulation, and self-interest. Named after the Italian Renaissance diplomat and political theorist Niccolò Machiavelli, this trait embodies a pragmatic and often ruthless approach to achieving one's goals. Individuals high in Machiavellianism tend to view others as tools to be used for personal gain, prioritizing their own success over ethical considerations or the well-being of others.

At its core, Machiavellianism involves a strategic and calculating mindset. Those who exhibit this trait are adept at reading social situations and understanding the motivations of others. They use this insight to craft intricate plans and manipulate circumstances to their advantage. Machiavellian individuals are often described as master tacticians, able to anticipate potential obstacles and devise complex strategies to overcome them.

One of the key aspects of Machiavellianism is the willingness to engage in deception and manipulation. Machiavellian individuals have no qualms about lying, cheating, or misleading others if it serves their purposes. They view honesty and transparency as potential weaknesses that can be exploited by others, and instead opt for a more guarded and calculated approach to interpersonal interactions. This propensity for deceit allows them to maintain control over situations and people, always keeping their true intentions hidden.

The Machiavellian personality is characterized by emotional detachment and a lack of empathy. These individuals are able to separate their emotions from their actions, allowing them to make decisions based solely on what will benefit them the most. This emotional distance enables them to manipulate others without feeling guilt or remorse, as they view relationships primarily as transactional rather than emotional connections.

Machiavellian individuals are skilled at identifying and exploiting the weaknesses of others. They possess a keen understanding of human psychology and use this knowledge to their advantage. By recognizing insecurities, desires, and vulnerabilities in those around them, they can craft tailored approaches to influence and control others. This ability to exploit weaknesses makes them particularly adept at navigating complex social and professional environments.

Another hallmark of Machiavellianism is the focus on long-term strategic thinking. While they may engage in short-term manipulations, Machiavellian individuals are always considering the bigger picture and how their actions will impact their future goals. They are patient and willing to bide their time, sometimes sacrificing immediate gains for greater rewards down the line. This long-term perspective allows them to build intricate networks of influence and power over time.

Machiavellianism is often associated with a cynical worldview. Those high in this trait tend to believe that most people are inherently selfish and untrustworthy. This cynicism fuels their belief that manipulation and deceit are necessary tools for survival and success in a cutthroat world. They view moral considerations as naïve and potentially dangerous, preferring instead to focus on pragmatic solutions that prioritize their own interests.

In professional settings, Machiavellian individuals are often drawn to positions of power and influence. They excel in roles that require strategic thinking, negotiation, and the ability to navigate complex social dynamics. Their willingness to make difficult decisions without being hindered by emotional considerations can make them effective leaders in certain contexts. However, their tendency to prioritize personal gain over the well-being of others can also lead to toxic work environments and damaged relationships.

The manipulative nature of Machiavellianism extends to how these individuals present themselves to others. They are skilled at crafting personas and adapting their behavior to suit different situations and audiences. This chameleon-like ability allows them to blend into various social contexts and gain the trust of those around them. By presenting a carefully curated image, they can disarm potential opponents and create opportunities for manipulation.

One of the key strategies employed by Machiavellian individuals is the use of charm and flattery. They understand the power of making others feel important and valued, and use this knowledge to build alliances and gain favor. However, this charm is always calculated and serves a specific purpose. Machiavellian individuals are not interested in genuine connections but rather in creating a network of people who can be useful to them in achieving their goals.

The concept of power is central to Machiavellianism. Those high in this trait are constantly seeking ways to increase their influence and control over others and their environment. They view power not just as an end in itself, but as a means to secure their position and achieve their objectives. This pursuit of power often leads them to engage in political maneuvering, alliance-building, and strategic positioning within social and professional hierarchies.

Machiavellian individuals are adept at information control. They understand that knowledge is power and are skilled at gathering intelligence while revealing as little about themselves as possible. This information asymmetry allows them to maintain an advantage in negotiations and interpersonal interactions. They are also skilled at using selective disclosure of information to manipulate perceptions and influence outcomes.

The ability to remain calm under pressure is another characteristic of Machiavellianism. These individuals are able to maintain their composure and strategic thinking even in high-stress situations. This coolness under fire allows them to outmaneuver opponents who may be more emotionally reactive. It also enables them to seize opportunities that others might miss due to anxiety or uncertainty.

While Machiavellianism can lead to personal success in certain contexts, it often comes at a significant cost to interpersonal relationships and ethical standing. The manipulative and self-serving nature of this trait can lead to a lack of genuine connections and a reputation for untrustworthiness. Over time, the actions of a Machiavellian individual may catch up with them, leading to social isolation and professional consequences.

It's important to note that Machiavellianism exists on a spectrum, and most people exhibit some degree of these traits. However, those high in Machiavellianism take these tendencies to an extreme, consistently prioritizing personal gain over other considerations. Understanding Machiavellianism is crucial for recognizing and navigating interactions with individuals who exhibit these traits, as well as for developing strategies to protect oneself from manipulation and deceit.

Historical Origins

Niccolò Machiavelli's seminal work, "The Prince," published posthumously in 1532, stands as a cornerstone in the development of political theory and the concept of Machiavellianism. This treatise, written as a guide for rulers, particularly new princes, has had a profound impact on both political thought and interpersonal relationships, shaping the understanding of power dynamics and strategic manipulation.

Machiavelli wrote "The Prince" during a tumultuous period in Italian history, characterized by political instability and frequent power shifts. Drawing from his experiences as a diplomat and his observations of successful and failed rulers, Machiavelli sought to provide practical advice for maintaining power in a chaotic world.

His approach was revolutionary for its time, as it departed from the idealistic and moralistic political philosophies that had dominated Western thought for centuries.

The core of Machiavelli's philosophy in "The Prince" is the notion that the ends justify the means. He argued that a ruler's primary goal should be the preservation and expansion of power, even if it requires actions that might be considered immoral or unethical by conventional standards. This pragmatic approach to governance was a stark departure from the prevailing Christian and humanist ideals of virtuous leadership.

Machiavelli's work introduced several key concepts that would later become central to the understanding of Machiavellianism. One of the most notable is the idea that it is better for a ruler to be feared than loved. He argued that while both fear and love can inspire loyalty, fear is more reliable because it stems from the dread of punishment, which is always in the prince's control. Love, on the other hand, is fickle and can easily turn to hatred if the people feel betrayed or disappointed.

Another crucial aspect of Machiavelli's philosophy is the emphasis on appearance over reality. He advised rulers to cultivate an image of virtue and morality while being prepared to act against these principles when necessary for the state's benefit. This concept of maintaining a facade while pursuing one's true objectives would become a hallmark of Machiavellian behavior in both political and interpersonal contexts.

Machiavelli also stressed the importance of adaptability and cunning in leadership. He argued that successful rulers must be able to change their behavior and tactics according to the circumstances, rather than adhering rigidly to a single approach. This flexibility, combined with a keen understanding of human nature and the ability to manipulate others, forms the foundation of Machiavellian strategy.

The impact of "The Prince" on political thought was immediate and long-lasting. While some contemporaries praised Machiavelli's realistic approach to politics, others condemned the work as immoral and dangerous. The Catholic Church placed "The Prince" on its Index of Prohibited Books in 1559, further fueling controversy and interest in Machiavelli's ideas.

Over time, Machiavelli's name became synonymous with cunning, deceit, and the ruthless pursuit of power. The term "Machiavellian" entered the English language in the 16th century, initially used to describe unscrupulous politicians and later applied more broadly to individuals who exhibited similar traits in their personal relationships.

The concept of Machiavellianism in psychology emerged in the 20th century, drawing heavily on the principles outlined in "The Prince." Psychologists Richard Christie and Florence Geis developed the MACH-IV test in 1970 to measure Machiavellian personality traits, including cynicism, emotional detachment, and a willingness to manipulate others for personal gain. This work helped establish Machiavellianism as one of the components of the Dark Triad of personality traits, alongside narcissism and psychopathy.

In politics, the influence of Machiavelli's ideas can be seen in the strategies and behaviors of numerous leaders throughout history. From the realpolitik of Otto von Bismarck to the power plays of modern politicians, Machiavellian principles continue to shape political maneuvering and decision-making. The concept of "political realism," which emphasizes the pursuit of national interests over moral considerations in international relations, owes much to Machiavelli's pragmatic approach to statecraft.

Beyond the realm of politics, Machiavellianism has found application in various fields, including business, negotiation, and interpersonal relationships. In the corporate world, Machiavellian tactics are often associated with office politics, strategic networking, and climbing the corporate ladder. While such behaviors are generally viewed negatively, some argue that a degree of

Machiavellianism can be beneficial in competitive environments.

In interpersonal relationships, Machiavellianism manifests as a tendency to manipulate and exploit others for personal gain. Individuals high in Machiavellian traits often excel at reading and influencing others, using charm and deception to achieve their goals. While these skills can lead to short-term success, they often result in shallow and unstable relationships, as others become wary of the Machiavellian individual's true motives.

The enduring influence of Machiavelli's work is a testament to its insight into human nature and power dynamics. While "The Prince" was written as a guide for political leaders, its principles have proven applicable to a wide range of human interactions. The concept of Machiavellianism continues to evolve, with ongoing research in psychology, sociology, and political science exploring its manifestations and implications in various contexts.

It is important to note that while Machiavelli's ideas have been influential, they have also been subject to criticism and reinterpretation. Some scholars argue that "The Prince" should be read as a satire or a warning against tyranny, rather than a straightforward manual for ruthless leadership. Others emphasize the importance of considering Machiavelli's other works, such as "Discourses on Livy," which present a more republican and civic-minded perspective on governance.

Regardless of these debates, the impact of "The Prince" on the concept of Machiavellianism is undeniable. Machiavelli's frank discussion of power, manipulation, and strategic thinking has provided a framework for understanding and analyzing human behavior in various spheres of life. As society continues to grapple with questions of leadership, ethics, and interpersonal dynamics, the insights offered by Machiavelli's work remain relevant and thought-provoking.

Tactics of Manipulation

Machiavellian individuals are known for their cunning and manipulative nature, employing a wide array of tactics to achieve their goals. These strategies are often subtle, sophisticated, and highly effective in controlling and influencing others. At the core of Machiavellianism lies the ability to manipulate, and those who score high on this trait are particularly adept at using various methods to bend situations and people to their will.

One of the primary tactics employed by Machiavellian individuals is emotional manipulation. They are skilled at recognizing and exploiting the emotions of others, using this knowledge to their advantage. By understanding what motivates people emotionally, they can tailor their approach to elicit specific responses. For instance, they might feign empathy or concern to gain trust, only to use that trust later for their own benefit. They may also play on people's insecurities, fears, or desires to manipulate them into certain actions or decisions. This emotional manipulation can be particularly insidious because it often goes unnoticed by the victim, who may believe they are acting of their own free will.

Lying is another cornerstone of Machiavellian manipulation. Those high in Machiavellianism have no qualms about dishonesty and view it as a necessary tool for achieving their objectives. They are often skilled liars, able to craft convincing falsehoods and maintain them over time. Their lies can range from small, seemingly insignificant untruths to elaborate fabrications designed to deceive on a grand scale. What sets Machiavellian liars apart is their ability to lie without guilt or remorse, viewing it as a pragmatic means to an end rather than a moral failing.

Closely related to lying is the tactic of deception. While lying involves actively telling untruths, deception can be more nuanced and multifaceted. Machiavellian individuals might use half-truths, omissions, or misleading information to create false impressions without technically lying. They may also engage in more complex forms of deception, such as creating false narratives or manipulating situations to mislead others. This can include staging events, planting false evidence, or orchestrating scenarios that lead others to draw incorrect conclusions.

Gaslighting is a particularly insidious form of manipulation favored by those high in Machiavellianism. This tactic involves making others question their own perceptions, memories, or sanity. By consistently denying or distorting reality, Machiavellian individuals can erode their victims' confidence and make them more susceptible to manipulation. This can involve denying events that occurred, rewriting history, or subtly altering the environment to create doubt and confusion.

Another tactic frequently employed is the use of flattery and charm. Machiavellian individuals are often charismatic and know how to use praise and compliments to win people over. They may lavish attention and admiration on their targets, making them feel special and valued. However, this charm is typically superficial and serves only to further the Machiavellian's agenda. Once they have achieved their goal, the charm may quickly disappear, leaving their victims feeling used and confused.

Divide and conquer is a strategy that Machiavellian individuals often use in group settings. By creating or exploiting divisions within a group, they can weaken opposition and increase their own power. This might involve spreading rumors, playing people against each other, or strategically sharing information to create conflict. By keeping others off-balance and focused on internal strife, the Machiavellian can more easily manipulate the situation to their advantage.

Machiavellian individuals are also adept at using information as a weapon. They may hoard knowledge, selectively share information, or use their access to information as leverage. By controlling the flow of information, they can shape narratives, influence decisions, and maintain power. This tactic can be particularly effective in professional settings where information is currency.

Another manipulation tactic is the creation of false choices or illusions of control. Machiavellian individuals may present limited options to their targets, all of which serve the Machiavellian's interests. This creates the illusion of choice while actually manipulating the outcome. Similarly, they may give others the impression of having control or input in a situation when, in reality, the Machiavellian is pulling the strings behind the scenes.

Guilt and obligation are powerful tools in the Machiavellian arsenal. They may do favors or provide assistance, not out of genuine altruism, but to create a sense of indebtedness in others. This can then be leveraged later to extract favors or compliance. Similarly, they may use guilt to manipulate others into action, making them feel responsible for situations or outcomes that are not truly their fault.

Machiavellian individuals often employ the tactic of strategic self-disclosure. They may share personal information or vulnerabilities to create a false sense of intimacy or trust. However, this openness is carefully calculated and serves to manipulate rather than to form genuine connections. They may also use this tactic to gather information about others, which can be used for future manipulation.

Another manipulation strategy is the use of social proof and peer pressure. Machiavellian individuals may create the impression that certain behaviors or decisions are widely accepted or expected, even when they are not. This can pressure others into conformity or compliance. They may also use social hierarchies to their advantage, aligning themselves with influential individuals or groups to increase their own power and credibility.

Machiavellian manipulators are often skilled at exploiting cognitive biases and psychological vulnerabilities. They may use techniques such as anchoring (providing a reference point to influence subsequent judgments), framing (presenting information in a way that influences interpretation), or the foot-in-the-door technique (starting with a small request to increase compliance with larger requests later). By understanding these psychological principles, they can subtly influence decision-making and behavior.

The use of intermittent reinforcement is another tactic employed by Machiavellian individuals. By alternating between positive and negative treatment, they can create a sense of unpredictability that keeps others off-balance and seeking approval. This can be particularly effective in creating emotional dependence and maintaining control over others.

It's important to note that while these tactics are often associated with Machiavellianism, they are not exclusive to this trait. Many people may use some of these strategies to varying degrees in their daily lives. What sets Machiavellian individuals apart is their willingness to use these tactics extensively, their skill in applying them, and their lack of moral qualms about manipulating others for personal gain. Understanding these tactics can help individuals recognize when they are being manipulated and develop strategies to protect themselves from Machiavellian influence.

The Machiavellian Leader

Throughout history, leaders who embody Machiavellian traits have left indelible marks on the world stage, shaping nations, economies, and societies through their cunning and strategic manipulation. These individuals, driven by an insatiable desire for power and influence, have often employed tactics that align closely with Machiavelli's principles outlined in "The Prince." By examining both historical and contemporary figures who exhibit these characteristics, we can gain valuable insights into the practical application of Machiavellianism in leadership roles.

One of the most notorious historical figures often associated with Machiavellianism is Napoleon Bonaparte. The French military and political leader's rise to power exemplifies many Machiavellian principles. Napoleon's ability to manipulate public opinion, exploit political rivalries, and strategically form alliances allowed him to consolidate power and establish a vast empire. His pragmatic approach to governance, which often prioritized expediency over morality, mirrors Machiavelli's advice to rulers. Napoleon's willingness to use force when necessary, coupled with his charismatic public image, demonstrates the complex interplay of fear and admiration that Machiavelli deemed essential for effective leadership.

In the realm of business, few figures embody Machiavellian traits as prominently as John D. Rockefeller. The oil tycoon's ruthless business practices and strategic maneuvering in the late 19th and early 20th centuries led to the creation of Standard Oil, one of the most powerful monopolies in American history. Rockefeller's tactics, which included predatory pricing, secret rebates, and industrial espionage, reflect the Machiavellian principle of using any means necessary to achieve one's goals. His ability to manipulate market conditions and eliminate competition showcases the effectiveness of Machiavellian strategies in the business world, even as they raised ethical concerns and eventually led to antitrust legislation.

Moving into the 20th century, Joseph Stalin's reign over the Soviet Union provides a chilling example of Machiavellianism in political leadership. Stalin's rise to power and subsequent rule were characterized by ruthless elimination of opponents, strategic alliances, and the cultivation of a powerful cult of personality. His ability to manipulate party politics, exploit ideological divisions, and maintain control through fear and propaganda aligns closely with Machiavellian principles. Stalin's pragmatic approach to foreign policy, including the Molotov-Ribbentrop Pact with Nazi Germany, further illustrates the Machiavellian emphasis on expediency over moral considerations in pursuit of power and national interests.

In the corporate world of the late 20th and early 21st centuries, Jack Welch, former CEO of General Electric, has been both praised and criticized for his Machiavellian approach to business leadership. Welch's tenure at GE was marked by aggressive cost-cutting measures, strategic acquisitions, and a ruthless performance-based culture. His famous "rank and yank" policy, which involved annually firing the bottom 10% of performers, exemplifies the Machiavellian principle of maintaining power through fear and competition. Welch's ability to dramatically increase GE's market value while cultivating a public image as a visionary leader demonstrates the potential effectiveness of Machiavellian tactics in modern corporate environments.

The political landscape of the 21st century has seen its fair share of leaders exhibiting Machiavellian traits. Vladimir Putin, the long-standing Russian president, has consistently demonstrated a mastery of Machiavellian tactics in both domestic and international politics. Putin's ability to consolidate power, suppress opposition, and project strength on the global stage aligns closely with Machiavellian principles. His strategic use of information warfare, including disinformation campaigns and cyber operations, showcases a modern application of Machiavelli's emphasis on perception management and the manipulation of truth for political gain.

In the tech industry, Steve Jobs, co-founder and former CEO of Apple, embodied many Machiavellian traits in his leadership style. Jobs was known for his charismatic yet often ruthless approach to product development and company management. His ability to create a "reality distortion field," manipulating perceptions and inspiring unwavering loyalty among employees and consumers alike, reflects the Machiavellian emphasis on the power of image and persuasion. Jobs' strategic decision-making, which often prioritized his vision over immediate market demands or employee comfort, demonstrates the Machiavellian principle of maintaining unwavering focus on long-term goals, regardless of short-term costs.

In the world of finance, hedge fund manager Ray Dalio has gained recognition for his application of Machiavellian principles in investment strategy and organizational management. Dalio's approach, which he terms "radical transparency," involves fostering a culture of constant critique and evaluation within his firm, Bridgewater Associates. This system, while ostensibly aimed at improving decision-making, also serves to maintain Dalio's control and influence over the organization. His emphasis on meritocracy and performance-based advancement aligns with Machiavellian ideas about rewarding competence and eliminating weakness, creating a highly competitive internal environment that mirrors Machiavelli's views on effective governance.

The rise of populist leaders in recent years has provided numerous examples of Machiavellianism in contemporary politics. Figures like Jair Bolsonaro in Brazil and Rodrigo Duterte in the Philippines have employed Machiavellian tactics to gain and maintain power. Their use of divisive rhetoric, strategic alliances with powerful interest groups, and willingness to challenge established norms and institutions reflect Machiavelli's advice on seizing and consolidating authority. These leaders' ability to cultivate a strong base of support while polarizing the broader population demonstrates the enduring relevance of Machiavellian strategies in modern democratic systems.

In the corporate world, Jeff Bezos, founder of Amazon, has displayed Machiavellian traits in his relentless pursuit of market dominance. Bezos' strategic decisions, including aggressive pricing strategies, vertical integration, and the cultivation of a data-driven, high-pressure work culture, align with Machiavellian principles of maintaining competitive advantage through any means necessary. His ability to anticipate and shape market trends, often at the expense of established industries and smaller competitors, showcases the effectiveness of Machiavellian foresight and adaptability in the rapidly evolving digital economy.

These examples, spanning different eras and sectors, illustrate the pervasive influence of Machiavellianism in leadership roles. While the specific tactics and contexts may vary, the core principles of strategic manipulation, pragmatic decision-making, and the relentless pursuit of power remain consistent. The effectiveness of these leaders in achieving their goals underscores the potency of Machiavellian approaches, even as it raises important ethical questions about the nature of leadership and the balance between individual ambition and societal well-being. As we continue to navigate complex political and economic landscapes, understanding the manifestations of Machiavellianism in leadership remains crucial for both recognizing its influence and developing appropriate responses to its challenges.

Chapter 3: The Face of Psychopathy

What is Psychopathy?

Psychopathy is a complex personality disorder characterized by a distinct set of behavioral and emotional traits that significantly deviate from societal norms. At its core, psychopathy is defined by a profound lack of empathy, shallow emotional experiences, superficial charm, and impulsive tendencies. These key features combine to create a unique and often troubling psychological profile that has captivated researchers, clinicians, and the general public for decades.

The lack of empathy is perhaps the most defining characteristic of psychopathy. Individuals with this disorder struggle to understand or relate to the emotions of others, often appearing cold and detached in situations that would typically elicit strong emotional responses from most people. This absence of empathy extends beyond mere indifference; psychopaths may actively exploit others' emotions for personal gain, viewing them as tools to be manipulated rather than as fellow human beings deserving of consideration and respect.

This empathic deficit is closely tied to the shallow emotional experiences that psychopaths typically report. While they may be able to mimic appropriate emotional responses in social situations, their internal emotional landscape is often described as barren or muted. Psychopaths rarely experience the full depth and richness of emotions that most individuals take for granted. Joy, sadness, fear, and love are often reduced to fleeting sensations or intellectual concepts rather than deeply felt experiences. This emotional shallowness contributes to their difficulty in forming meaningful relationships and their tendency to engage in risky or antisocial behaviors without consideration for the consequences.

Superficial charm is another hallmark of psychopathy, often serving as a mask to conceal the disorder's more troubling aspects. Psychopaths can be exceptionally charismatic and adept at social interactions, using their charm to manipulate and deceive others. They may appear confident, witty, and engaging, easily drawing people into their orbit. However, this charm is ultimately hollow, lacking the genuine warmth and connection that typically underpin healthy social relationships. Instead, it serves as a tool for the psychopath to achieve their goals, whether those involve financial gain, social status, or simply the thrill of successfully duping others.

Impulsivity rounds out the core features of psychopathy, manifesting as a tendency to act on immediate desires without consideration for long-term consequences or the impact on others. This trait often leads psychopaths to engage in risky or criminal behaviors, as they struggle to delay gratification or adhere to societal norms and laws. The impulsive nature of psychopaths can make them unpredictable and potentially dangerous, as they may react with sudden aggression or make rash decisions that harm themselves or others.

It is important to note that psychopathy exists on a spectrum, with individuals exhibiting these traits to varying degrees. Not all psychopaths are violent criminals, and many may function within society, albeit often leaving a trail of emotional devastation in their wake. The severity and combination of these key features can result in different manifestations of the disorder, ranging from highly successful individuals in positions of power to chronic offenders unable to maintain stability in any area of their lives.

The origins of psychopathy remain a subject of ongoing research and debate within the scientific community. While there is evidence to suggest a genetic component to the disorder, environmental factors such as childhood trauma, neglect, or inconsistent parenting are also believed to play a role in its development. The complex interplay between nature and nurture in shaping psychopathic traits continues to be a focus of study, with implications for both treatment approaches and our understanding of human psychology more broadly.

Diagnosing psychopathy presents unique challenges due to the manipulative nature of those with the disorder and their ability to present a façade of normalcy. Clinical assessment tools such as the Psychopathy Checklist-Revised (PCL-R) have been developed to aid in identification, but these require skilled administration and interpretation. The PCL-R evaluates individuals across twenty items that correspond to the key features of psychopathy, providing a standardized method for assessing the presence and severity of psychopathic traits.

The impact of psychopathy extends far beyond the individuals who possess the disorder. Families, romantic partners, colleagues, and entire communities can be profoundly affected by the actions of psychopaths. The emotional toll on those who have been manipulated or victimized by individuals with psychopathy can be severe and long-lasting, often requiring therapeutic intervention to overcome.

In professional settings, psychopaths may rise to positions of power due to their charm and willingness to take risks, potentially creating toxic work environments and engaging in unethical business practices. In personal relationships, they may leave a wake of emotional destruction, moving from one partner to another without genuine attachment or remorse.

The criminal justice system grapples with the challenges posed by psychopathic offenders, who are often overrepresented in prison populations and show higher rates of recidivism compared to non-psychopathic criminals. The lack of empathy and remorse characteristic of psychopathy makes rehabilitation particularly challenging, raising difficult questions about the most effective ways to protect society while addressing the underlying disorder.

Research into psychopathy continues to evolve, with new insights emerging from fields such as neuroscience and genetics. Brain imaging studies have revealed structural and functional differences in the brains of individuals with psychopathy, particularly in areas associated with emotion processing and impulse control. These findings offer tantalizing clues about the biological underpinnings of the disorder and may eventually lead to new approaches for intervention and treatment.

As our understanding of psychopathy deepens, so too does the complexity of the ethical and philosophical questions it raises. The disorder challenges our notions of free will, moral responsibility, and the nature of human emotion. It forces us to confront uncomfortable truths about the capacity for cruelty and indifference that exists within the human psyche, while also highlighting the profound importance of empathy and emotional connection in shaping a functional society.

The Neuroscience of Psychopathy

The neuroscience of psychopathy has been a subject of intense research and fascination for scientists and clinicians alike. By examining the brain structures and neurological differences in individuals with psychopathic traits, researchers have gained valuable insights into the underlying mechanisms that contribute to this complex personality disorder. Two key areas of the brain that have been consistently implicated in psychopathy are the amygdala and the prefrontal cortex.

The amygdala, an almond-shaped structure located deep within the temporal lobes of the brain, plays a crucial role in emotional processing, fear conditioning, and the recognition of emotional expressions in others. In psychopathic individuals, studies have consistently shown reduced amygdala volume and diminished activity in response to emotional stimuli, particularly those related to fear and distress. This abnormality in amygdala function may explain the characteristic lack of empathy and emotional callousness observed in psychopaths, as they struggle to recognize and respond appropriately to others' emotional cues.

Functional neuroimaging studies have revealed that psychopaths exhibit reduced amygdala activation when presented with emotionally charged stimuli, such as images of facial expressions depicting fear or distress. This diminished response suggests that psychopaths may have difficulty processing and interpreting emotional information, leading to their apparent indifference to the suffering of others. Additionally, the reduced amygdala activity may contribute to their impaired ability to learn from punishment and their tendency to engage in risky or antisocial behaviors without considering the potential consequences.

The prefrontal cortex, located at the front of the brain, is responsible for executive functions such as decision-making, impulse control, and moral reasoning. In psychopathic individuals, researchers have observed structural and functional abnormalities in various regions of the prefrontal cortex, particularly the orbitofrontal cortex and the ventromedial prefrontal cortex. These areas are crucial for regulating emotions, making moral judgments, and inhibiting inappropriate behaviors.

Neuroimaging studies have shown reduced gray matter volume in the prefrontal cortex of psychopathic individuals, which may contribute to their impaired decision-making abilities and lack of impulse control. Furthermore, functional MRI studies have revealed decreased activation in the prefrontal cortex during tasks that require moral reasoning or the consideration of long-term consequences. This reduced activity may explain why psychopaths often engage in impulsive and antisocial behaviors without regard for the potential negative outcomes or the impact on others.

The connectivity between the amygdala and the prefrontal cortex is also disrupted in psychopathic individuals. This impaired communication between these two critical brain regions may result in a failure to integrate emotional information with cognitive processes, leading to deficits in moral decision-making and empathy. The disconnection between these areas may explain why psychopaths can understand the concept of right and wrong on an intellectual level but fail to internalize or act upon these moral principles in their daily lives.

Another brain region that has been implicated in psychopathy is the anterior cingulate cortex (ACC). The ACC is involved in error detection, conflict monitoring, and the regulation of emotional responses. Studies have shown reduced ACC activation in psychopathic individuals during tasks that require emotional processing or the recognition of errors. This abnormality may contribute to their difficulty in learning from mistakes and their tendency to persist in maladaptive behaviors despite negative consequences.

Researchers have also identified differences in the white matter tracts that connect various brain regions in psychopathic individuals. Diffusion tensor imaging studies have revealed reduced integrity of the uncinate fasciculus, a white matter tract that connects the amygdala and the prefrontal cortex. This structural abnormality may further contribute to the impaired communication between these two critical brain regions, exacerbating the emotional and behavioral deficits observed in psychopathy.

The neurotransmitter systems in the brains of psychopathic individuals have also been a subject of investigation. Studies have found alterations in the serotonin system, which is involved in mood regulation, impulse control, and aggression. Psychopathic individuals have been shown to have reduced serotonin function, which may contribute to their increased aggression and impulsivity. Additionally, abnormalities in the dopamine system, which is involved in reward processing and motivation, have been observed in psychopathic individuals. These alterations may explain their tendency to seek out novel and exciting experiences, often at the expense of others or societal norms.

It is important to note that while these neurological differences are consistently observed in psychopathic individuals, the relationship between brain structure and function and psychopathic behavior is complex and multifaceted. Environmental factors, such as childhood experiences and social influences, also play a significant role in the development and expression of psychopathic traits. The interaction between genetic predisposition and environmental factors likely contributes to the wide range of psychopathic behaviors observed in clinical and forensic settings.

Recent advances in neuroimaging techniques and genetic research have provided new avenues for investigating the neurobiology of psychopathy. Genome-wide association studies have identified several genetic variants that may be associated with psychopathic traits, offering potential insights into the heritability of this disorder. Additionally, new neuroimaging methods, such as multimodal imaging and machine learning approaches, are allowing researchers to examine the complex interactions between different brain regions and networks in psychopathic individuals with unprecedented detail.

Understanding the neuroscience of psychopathy has important implications for both clinical practice and the criminal justice system. By identifying the neural correlates of psychopathic traits, researchers may be able to develop more targeted interventions and treatment strategies for individuals with psychopathic tendencies. Furthermore, this knowledge may inform legal and ethical discussions surrounding the culpability and rehabilitation of psychopathic offenders.

As research in this field continues to evolve, it is becoming increasingly clear that psychopathy is a complex disorder with deep roots in brain structure and function. While much progress has been made in understanding the neuroscience of psychopathy, many questions remain unanswered. Future research will undoubtedly continue to shed light on the intricate relationship between brain function and psychopathic behavior, potentially leading to more effective prevention and intervention strategies for this challenging and often devastating personality disorder.

Psychopathy vs. Sociopathy

The terms psychopathy and sociopathy are often used interchangeably in popular culture, leading to confusion about their distinct characteristics. While both fall under the umbrella of antisocial personality disorders, they possess unique features that set them apart. Understanding these differences is crucial for professionals in psychology, law enforcement, and related fields, as well as for individuals seeking to comprehend the complexities of these personality disorders.

Psychopathy is generally considered to have a stronger genetic component, with research suggesting that certain neurological differences may predispose individuals to develop psychopathic traits. These differences often manifest in reduced activity in the amygdala, the brain region responsible for processing emotions, particularly fear and anxiety. This neurological variance contributes to the hallmark characteristics of psychopathy, such as a lack of empathy, shallow emotions, and fearlessness.

Sociopathy, on the other hand, is believed to be more heavily influenced by environmental factors. Traumatic experiences, abuse, neglect, or exposure to violence during childhood can contribute to the development of sociopathic traits. While genetic factors may play a role, the emphasis on environmental influences distinguishes sociopathy from psychopathy in terms of its origins.

Both psychopaths and sociopaths exhibit antisocial behaviors and a disregard for social norms and the rights of others. However, the manner in which these traits manifest can differ significantly. Psychopaths tend to be more calculating, manipulative, and adept at masking their true nature. They often possess superficial charm and can be highly skilled at mimicking emotions to blend in with society. This ability to camouflage their true selves allows many psychopaths to maintain successful careers and relationships, at least on the surface.

Sociopaths, in contrast, may struggle more with impulse control and have difficulty maintaining a facade of normalcy. Their antisocial behaviors are often more erratic and impulsive, making it challenging for them to sustain long-term relationships or hold steady employment. While both psychopaths and sociopaths may engage in criminal activities, sociopaths are more likely to act on impulse, potentially leading to less sophisticated and more easily detectable crimes.

The emotional landscape of psychopaths and sociopaths also differs in subtle but important ways. Psychopaths are often described as having a complete lack of empathy and conscience. They may understand the concept of right and wrong on an intellectual level but feel no emotional connection to these moral principles. This emotional void allows them to commit heinous acts without remorse or guilt.

Sociopaths, while also displaying reduced empathy, may retain some capacity for emotional connection, particularly with a select few individuals. They might experience fleeting moments of guilt or shame, although these emotions are typically short-lived and do not significantly impact their behavior. Sociopaths may also exhibit more volatile emotions, prone to outbursts of anger or frustration when their desires are thwarted.

The ability to form relationships presents another area of divergence between psychopathy and sociopathy. Psychopaths are often skilled at creating superficial connections and can be quite charming in social situations. They may have numerous acquaintances and even long-term partners, but these relationships lack depth and genuine emotional attachment. Psychopaths view others primarily as tools to be used for personal gain or entertainment.

Sociopaths, due to their more impulsive nature and difficulty in maintaining a consistent facade, may struggle to form and maintain relationships. They may have a small circle of individuals they feel connected to, but these relationships are often tumultuous and marked by frequent conflicts. Sociopaths may experience a form of loyalty to these select few, albeit in a distorted and self-serving manner.

In terms of criminal behavior, both psychopaths and sociopaths are overrepresented in prison populations compared to the general public. However, the nature of their crimes and their behavior within the criminal justice system can differ. Psychopaths are more likely to engage in premeditated, carefully planned crimes. Their lack of empathy and fear, combined with their manipulative skills, can make them particularly dangerous and difficult to rehabilitate.

Sociopaths, driven more by impulse and emotion, may commit crimes that are less organized and more reactive to immediate circumstances. Their criminal activities might be characterized by a greater degree of violence or recklessness. Within the prison system, sociopaths may struggle more with adhering to rules and may be more prone to conflicts with other inmates and staff.

The treatment approaches for psychopathy and sociopathy also reflect their distinct characteristics. Psychopathy is generally considered more resistant to treatment, partly due to the neurological differences underlying the condition. Traditional therapeutic approaches that rely on emotional engagement or appeals to empathy are often ineffective with psychopaths. Instead, treatment strategies may focus on behavior modification and creating external incentives for prosocial behavior.

Sociopathy, with its stronger environmental component, may be more amenable to certain forms of therapy. Cognitive-behavioral approaches that address impulsivity and emotional regulation can be beneficial. Additionally, interventions that focus on addressing underlying trauma or providing positive social support may help mitigate some sociopathic tendencies.

The legal system's approach to psychopathy and sociopathy also reflects their nuanced differences. While both conditions may be considered in criminal proceedings, the calculated nature of psychopathic crimes may lead to harsher sentences. The apparent lack of remorse displayed by psychopaths can also influence judicial decisions. Sociopaths, whose crimes may be more impulsive, might be viewed differently by the legal system, potentially leading to considerations of diminished capacity in some cases.

Research into psychopathy and sociopathy continues to evolve, with new insights emerging from fields such as neuroscience and genetics. These advancements are helping to refine our understanding of the distinctions between these two conditions and may lead to more targeted interventions and treatment approaches in the future.

Understanding the differences between psychopathy and sociopathy is crucial not only for professionals in mental health and criminal justice but also for society at large. Recognizing the unique characteristics of each condition can aid in early identification, inform prevention strategies, and guide the development of more effective treatment and management approaches. While both psychopathy and sociopathy present significant challenges, a nuanced understanding of their similarities and differences is essential for addressing the complex issues they pose to individuals and society.

Psychopaths in Society

Psychopaths have long been a subject of fascination and concern in society, often portrayed as dangerous criminals in media and popular culture. However, the reality of psychopathy is far more complex and nuanced. While some psychopaths do engage in criminal behavior, many others navigate society without ever breaking the law. These individuals, often referred to as "successful psychopaths," can be found in various positions of power and influence across different sectors of society.

The concept of successful psychopathy challenges the traditional notion that psychopaths are inherently dysfunctional or destined for a life of crime. Instead, it suggests that certain psychopathic traits, when combined with other factors such as intelligence, charm, and ambition, can lead to significant achievements in professional and social spheres. These individuals may excel in fields that reward traits associated with psychopathy, such as fearlessness, charisma, and the ability to remain calm under pressure.

Corporate environments, in particular, have been identified as potential breeding grounds for successful psychopaths. The cutthroat nature of business, with its emphasis on competition, risk-taking, and profit maximization, can create an atmosphere where psychopathic traits are not only tolerated but sometimes even rewarded. Studies have suggested that the prevalence of psychopathic traits among corporate executives may be higher than in the general population, with some estimates ranging from 3% to 21%, depending on the specific industry and level of management.

In the corporate world, psychopaths may rise through the ranks by leveraging their charm, manipulative skills, and lack of empathy to outmaneuver colleagues and secure promotions. Their ability to make tough decisions without emotional interference can be seen as an asset in high-stakes business environments. However, their presence can also have detrimental effects on organizational culture, employee morale, and long-term company sustainability. The psychopath's tendency to prioritize personal gain over the well-being of others can lead to unethical business practices, financial fraud, and a toxic work environment.

The political arena is another domain where successful psychopaths may thrive. The qualities that can make a psychopath successful in business – charisma, fearlessness, and the ability to manipulate others – can also be advantageous in politics. Political psychopaths may be skilled at crafting compelling narratives, rallying supporters, and navigating complex power dynamics. Their lack of empathy and moral constraints can allow them to make decisions that others might find difficult, potentially leading to both positive and negative outcomes for their constituents.

However, the presence of psychopaths in positions of political power raises significant ethical concerns. Their tendency to prioritize personal gain over public welfare can result in policies that benefit a select few at the expense of the broader population. Additionally, their skill at manipulation and deceit can undermine democratic processes and erode public trust in institutions.

It is important to note that not all successful individuals in corporate or political settings are psychopaths, and not all psychopaths achieve success in these domains. The interplay between psychopathic traits and success is complex and influenced by various factors, including intelligence, education, social skills, and environmental circumstances. Some researchers argue that certain psychopathic traits, when present in moderation and balanced by other positive qualities, may contribute to leadership effectiveness and innovation.

The role of psychopaths in society extends beyond the corporate and political realms. In fields such as law enforcement, military operations, and high-risk professions, certain psychopathic traits like fearlessness and emotional detachment may be advantageous. These individuals might be better equipped to handle high-stress situations or make difficult decisions under pressure.

However, the potential benefits must be weighed against the risks associated with having individuals with limited empathy and moral constraints in positions of authority.

The impact of successful psychopaths on society is a subject of ongoing debate and research. While they may contribute to innovation, efficiency, and decisive leadership in certain contexts, their presence can also lead to widespread harm and societal dysfunction. The psychopath's disregard for social norms and ethical considerations can result in decisions that prioritize short-term gains over long-term sustainability, potentially leading to economic instability, environmental degradation, and social inequality.

Moreover, the success of psychopaths in various domains of society may have a broader cultural impact. As these individuals rise to positions of power and influence, they may shape societal values and norms in ways that align with their own psychopathic tendencies. This could potentially lead to a normalization of traits such as callousness, manipulation, and excessive self-interest, influencing how success is defined and pursued in society.

The challenge for society lies in developing systems and structures that can identify and mitigate the negative impacts of psychopaths in positions of power while still allowing for the potential benefits of their unique skill sets. This may involve implementing more robust ethical frameworks, enhancing accountability measures, and promoting leadership models that emphasize empathy, collaboration, and long-term sustainability.

Education and awareness also play crucial roles in addressing the impact of psychopaths in society. By improving public understanding of psychopathy and its manifestations, individuals and organizations can better recognize and respond to psychopathic behavior. This knowledge can inform hiring practices, leadership development programs, and governance structures to create environments that are less conducive to psychopathic manipulation and exploitation.

Research into successful psychopathy continues to evolve, challenging our understanding of the relationship between personality traits and societal outcomes. As we gain more insights into the complex interplay between psychopathy and success, we may be better equipped to harness the potential benefits of certain psychopathic traits while mitigating their harmful effects on individuals and society as a whole.

The presence of psychopaths in various sectors of society underscores the need for a nuanced approach to personality and behavior in professional and social contexts. While the traits associated with psychopathy can lead to significant achievements and innovations, they also pose substantial risks to organizational health, social cohesion, and ethical governance. Balancing these considerations remains a critical challenge for modern society as we navigate the complex landscape of human behavior and its impact on our collective well-being.

Chapter 4: The Interplay of the Dark Triad

Overlap of Traits

The Dark Triad traits of narcissism, Machiavellianism, and psychopathy are often discussed as distinct personality characteristics. However, research has consistently shown that these traits frequently overlap and coexist within individuals, creating a complex interplay of behaviors and thought patterns. This overlap is not merely coincidental but reflects the interconnected nature of these traits and how they can reinforce and amplify one another.

At the core of this overlap is a shared foundation of self-centeredness and disregard for others. Narcissists, Machiavellians, and psychopaths all exhibit a tendency to prioritize their own needs and desires above those of others. This common ground serves as a fertile soil for the development and expression of all three traits. For instance, a narcissist's inflated sense of self-importance can easily align with a Machiavellian's manipulative tendencies, as both serve to elevate the individual's status and achieve their goals at the expense of others.

The overlap between narcissism and psychopathy is particularly pronounced. Both traits involve a lack of empathy, albeit manifesting in different ways. Narcissists may struggle to empathize due to their intense focus on themselves, while psychopaths often lack the capacity for empathy altogether. This shared characteristic can lead to a reinforcing cycle where the absence of empathy fuels both narcissistic and psychopathic behaviors, making it difficult to distinguish between the two traits in some individuals.

Machiavellianism, with its emphasis on strategic thinking and manipulation, can act as a catalyst for both narcissistic and psychopathic tendencies. A Machiavellian individual may employ their cunning to feed a narcissist's need for admiration or to facilitate a psychopath's exploitative behaviors. In turn, the grandiosity of narcissism and the fearlessness of psychopathy can embolden Machiavellian strategies, creating a synergistic effect that amplifies all three traits.

The overlap of these traits often manifests in specific behavioral patterns. For example, an individual high in all three Dark Triad traits might exhibit a combination of charm, manipulation, and callousness in their interpersonal relationships. They may use their narcissistic charisma to attract others, their Machiavellian tactics to manipulate them, and their psychopathic lack of remorse to exploit them without hesitation. This potent combination can make such individuals particularly dangerous in both personal and professional contexts.

Research has shown that the Dark Triad traits share common developmental pathways, which may explain their frequent co-occurrence. Factors such as childhood experiences, genetic predispositions, and environmental influences can contribute to the development of all three traits simultaneously. For instance, a child raised in an environment that rewards self-promotion and disregard for others' feelings may develop narcissistic tendencies alongside Machiavellian strategies for getting ahead.

The interplay between these traits can also be observed in how they influence cognitive processes. Narcissism may lead to an overestimation of one's abilities, which in turn can fuel Machiavellian plotting and psychopathic risk-taking. The cold, analytical thinking associated with Machiavellianism can provide a framework for narcissistic self-aggrandizement and psychopathic disregard for consequences. Meanwhile, the impulsivity often seen in psychopathy can lead to rash actions that serve narcissistic needs for attention and Machiavellian desires for power.

In the realm of interpersonal relationships, the overlap of Dark Triad traits can create a particularly toxic dynamic. A person exhibiting all three traits may form relationships solely for personal gain, using narcissistic charm to attract partners, Machiavellian manipulation to control them, and psychopathic detachment to discard them when they no longer serve a purpose. This pattern of behavior can leave a trail of emotional destruction and eroded trust in its wake.

The workplace provides another arena where the overlap of Dark Triad traits becomes evident. An employee or leader high in all three traits might use their narcissistic confidence to climb the corporate ladder, their Machiavellian strategies to outmaneuver colleagues, and their psychopathic lack of empathy to make ruthless decisions without regard for the human cost. This combination can lead to short-term success but often results in long-term damage to organizational culture and employee well-being.

It's important to note that while these traits often overlap, the degree of overlap can vary significantly between individuals. Some may exhibit strong tendencies in one area with only mild manifestations in others, while others may show a more balanced distribution across all three traits. This variability adds to the complexity of understanding and addressing Dark Triad personalities in real-world settings.

The co-existence of these traits also poses challenges for treatment and intervention. Traditional therapeutic approaches may struggle to address the multifaceted nature of individuals high in all three Dark Triad traits. A narcissist's resistance to criticism, a Machiavellian's tendency to manipulate the therapeutic process, and a psychopath's lack of motivation to change can all hinder efforts at personal growth and behavioral modification.

Understanding the overlap and interplay of Dark Triad traits is crucial for researchers, clinicians, and anyone dealing with individuals who exhibit these characteristics. Recognizing that these traits often come as a package rather than in isolation can help in developing more comprehensive strategies for assessment, intervention, and management of Dark Triad personalities.

The study of Dark Triad trait overlap also raises intriguing questions about personality development and the nature of antisocial behavior. Are these traits truly distinct constructs that happen to co-occur, or are they different manifestations of a more fundamental underlying factor? Ongoing research in this area may shed light on the deeper structures of personality and the origins of socially aversive traits.

As our understanding of the Dark Triad evolves, it becomes increasingly clear that narcissism, Machiavellianism, and psychopathy are not isolated traits but interconnected aspects of a broader pattern of antisocial personality characteristics. Their tendency to overlap and reinforce one another creates a complex web of behaviors and attitudes that can have profound impacts on individuals and society. By continuing to explore the nuances of this interplay, we can hope to develop better strategies for identifying, managing, and potentially mitigating the negative effects of Dark Triad personalities in various contexts of human interaction.

The Synergy of the Dark Triad

The Dark Triad traits—Machiavellianism, narcissism, and psychopathy—are formidable on their own, but when combined, they create a particularly potent and dangerous personality constellation. This synergy amplifies the negative aspects of each trait, resulting in individuals who are exceptionally manipulative, callous, and ruthless. The interplay between these traits produces a unique set of behaviors and thought patterns that can be highly destructive to both the individual and those around them.

At the core of this synergy is the amplification of self-interest and disregard for others. Machiavellianism contributes strategic thinking and a willingness to manipulate, narcissism adds a grandiose sense of self and a need for admiration, while psychopathy brings emotional coldness and impulsivity. Together, these traits create individuals who are not only skilled at manipulation but also feel entitled to exploit others for their own gain, all while lacking empathy or remorse for their actions.

The manipulative nature of the Dark Triad is perhaps its most prominent feature. Machiavellian traits provide the strategic mindset and willingness to deceive, while narcissism fuels the confidence and charm needed to execute these manipulations effectively. Psychopathic traits contribute to the lack of moral constraints that might otherwise inhibit such behavior. This combination results in individuals who are exceptionally adept at identifying others' weaknesses and exploiting them for personal gain, often through elaborate schemes or long-term manipulation strategies.

The callousness exhibited by those high in Dark Triad traits is another key aspect of their dangerous nature. Psychopathy contributes significantly to this emotional coldness, but it is reinforced by the Machiavellian view of others as mere pawns and the narcissistic lack of empathy. This callousness allows Dark Triad individuals to inflict harm on others without experiencing guilt or remorse, making them particularly dangerous in positions of power or influence.

Ruthlessness is the third pillar of the Dark Triad's synergy. The combination of Machiavellian strategic thinking, narcissistic entitlement, and psychopathic impulsivity creates individuals who are willing to go to extreme lengths to achieve their goals. They may engage in sabotage, blackmail, or even violence without hesitation if they believe it will further their interests. This ruthlessness is often accompanied by a lack of fear of consequences, as the psychopathic traits dampen anxiety and the narcissistic traits foster a sense of invulnerability.

The synergy of the Dark Triad also manifests in a unique approach to interpersonal relationships. These individuals often view relationships solely in terms of what they can gain, rather than as genuine connections. They may cultivate a wide network of acquaintances and appear charming and likable on the surface, but these relationships are typically shallow and self-serving. The Machiavellian aspect allows them to maintain a façade of friendliness, while the narcissistic and psychopathic traits prevent them from forming deep emotional bonds.

In professional settings, the Dark Triad synergy can lead to particularly destructive behaviors. These individuals may rise quickly in organizations due to their charm, confidence, and willingness to do whatever it takes to succeed. However, their presence often creates a toxic work environment characterized by backstabbing, credit-stealing, and unethical decision-making. They may also engage in corporate psychopathy, making risky decisions that benefit them in the short term while potentially causing long-term harm to the organization.

The Dark Triad's influence on decision-making processes is another crucial aspect of its synergy. The combination of traits leads to a decision-making style that is both calculated and impulsive. The Machiavellian element contributes to long-term strategic planning, while the psychopathic impulsivity can lead to sudden, high-risk actions. This is further complicated by the narcissistic tendency to overestimate one's abilities and underestimate risks, resulting in decisions that can be both cunning and reckless.

The impact of the Dark Triad on emotional processing and expression is also significant. These individuals often display what psychologists call "emotional poverty," characterized by a limited range of emotional experiences and expressions. This emotional deficiency is primarily driven by the psychopathic traits but is reinforced by the Machiavellian tendency to view emotions as tools for manipulation and the narcissistic focus on the self. As a result, Dark Triad individuals may struggle to understand or relate to others' emotions, further contributing to their callousness and manipulative behaviors.

Another dangerous aspect of the Dark Triad synergy is its effect on moral reasoning. The combination of traits often results in a highly flexible moral code that bends to suit the individual's needs. Machiavellian traits contribute to moral relativism, where right and wrong are determined by what benefits the individual. Narcissistic entitlement leads to a belief that normal moral rules don't apply to them, while psychopathic traits reduce the emotional impact of moral transgressions. This moral flexibility allows Dark Triad individuals to justify almost any action, no matter how unethical or harmful.

The Dark Triad's influence extends to how these individuals perceive and interact with society at large. They often view social norms and laws as inconvenient obstacles rather than important guidelines for behavior. This attitude, combined with their manipulative skills and lack of empathy, can lead them to engage in a wide range of antisocial behaviors, from white-collar crime to more violent offenses. Their ability to charm and manipulate often allows them to avoid detection or consequences for their actions, further reinforcing their sense of being above societal rules.

The synergy of the Dark Triad also manifests in a unique relationship with power. These individuals are often drawn to positions of authority and influence, not out of a desire to lead or contribute positively, but because of the opportunities for personal gain and control over others.

Once in power, they may use their position to exploit subordinates, manipulate systems for personal benefit, and create a culture of fear and competition. This can lead to systemic issues in organizations and even broader societal problems when Dark Triad individuals attain high-level positions in government or industry.

It's important to note that while the Dark Triad represents a particularly dangerous combination of traits, not all individuals who exhibit these characteristics will engage in severely antisocial or criminal behavior. The expression of these traits exists on a spectrum, and environmental factors play a significant role in how they manifest. However, the potential for harm remains high, especially in situations where Dark Triad individuals are able to accumulate power and influence.

Understanding the synergy of the Dark Triad is crucial for psychology, criminology, and organizational behavior. It provides insights into the motivations and thought processes behind some of the most destructive human behaviors. This knowledge can be applied in various fields, from improving hiring practices to developing more effective interventions for individuals with these traits. It also highlights the importance of creating systems and cultures that can identify and mitigate the negative impacts of Dark Triad personalities.

Real-World Implications

The Dark Triad traits of narcissism, Machiavellianism, and psychopathy have significant implications in various real-world contexts. These personalities often manifest in ways that can profoundly impact organizations, political systems, and interpersonal relationships. By examining case studies across different domains, we can gain valuable insights into how individuals with Dark Triad traits operate and influence their environments.

In the business world, Dark Triad personalities can be both assets and liabilities. A notable case study is that of Enron's former CEO, Jeffrey Skilling. Skilling exhibited traits consistent with narcissism and psychopathy, which initially propelled him to great success. His charisma and confidence attracted investors and employees alike, while his lack of empathy allowed him to make ruthless decisions that temporarily boosted the company's performance. However, these same traits ultimately led to Enron's downfall. Skilling's grandiose sense of self and disregard for ethical considerations resulted in fraudulent accounting practices and a toxic corporate culture. This case illustrates how Dark Triad traits can drive short-term success but often lead to long-term catastrophe in the business world.

Another example from the corporate sphere is Steve Jobs, co-founder of Apple Inc. While Jobs was undoubtedly a visionary leader, he also displayed narcissistic tendencies. His perfectionism and unwavering belief in his ideas drove Apple to create revolutionary products. However, his narcissism also manifested in a demanding and sometimes abusive management style. Jobs' case demonstrates how Dark Triad traits, particularly narcissism, can coexist with genuine talent and innovation, producing both positive and negative outcomes in a business context.

In politics, Dark Triad personalities can have far-reaching consequences on entire nations. A compelling case study is that of Joseph Stalin, the former leader of the Soviet Union. Stalin's regime was characterized by extreme paranoia, ruthlessness, and a cult of personality – all hallmarks of Dark Triad traits. His Machiavellian approach to power allowed him to outmaneuver his rivals and consolidate control. Meanwhile, his psychopathic tendencies enabled him to order mass executions and forced labor camps without remorse. Stalin's rule demonstrates how Dark Triad traits in political leaders can lead to authoritarian regimes and widespread human rights abuses.

On a more contemporary note, former U.S. President Donald Trump has been the subject of numerous psychological analyses suggesting the presence of Dark

Triad traits. Trump's grandiose self-promotion and sensitivity to criticism align with narcissistic tendencies. His unconventional and often confrontational approach to diplomacy and governance could be interpreted as Machiavellian. Some observers have also noted a lack of empathy in his responses to various crises, a trait associated with psychopathy. The Trump presidency illustrates how Dark Triad personalities in modern democratic systems can polarize the electorate, challenge institutional norms, and reshape political discourse.

In personal relationships, individuals with Dark Triad traits can leave a trail of emotional destruction. A case study from the realm of romance is that of "Dirty John" Meehan, whose story gained widespread attention through a podcast and subsequent TV series. Meehan, who displayed strong psychopathic and Machiavellian traits, engaged in a pattern of deceiving and manipulating romantic partners. He used charm and calculated lies to gain the trust of his victims, exploited them financially, and resorted to threats and violence when confronted. This case highlights how Dark Triad individuals can be dangerously alluring in personal relationships, adept at manipulating emotions and exploiting vulnerabilities.

Family dynamics can also be severely impacted by Dark Triad personalities. Consider the case of Dr. Deborah Schurman-Kauflin, a criminal profiler who grew up with a psychopathic father. In her accounts, she describes a childhood marked by unpredictable violence, emotional manipulation, and a constant state of fear. Her father's lack of empathy, impulsivity, and sadistic tendencies created a toxic family environment that had lasting effects on all family members. This case underscores the profound and often intergenerational impact that Dark Triad traits can have within family units.

In the world of academia and scientific research, the case of Diederik Stapel provides insight into how Dark Triad traits can corrupt the pursuit of knowledge. Stapel, a former professor of social psychology, was found to have fabricated data in numerous published studies. His actions were driven by a combination of narcissistic desire for acclaim and Machiavellian willingness to deceive. The case shook the scientific community and highlighted how Dark Triad traits can undermine the integrity of research and the academic peer review process.

The entertainment industry offers numerous examples of Dark Triad personalities, with the case of Harvey Weinstein standing out for its far-reaching implications. Weinstein, a powerful film producer, exhibited traits consistent with all three Dark Triad components. His narcissistic sense of entitlement, Machiavellian manipulation of aspiring actors, and psychopathic disregard for the wellbeing of his victims allowed him to engage in a long-standing pattern of sexual abuse. The Weinstein case not only demonstrates the havoc

Dark Triad individuals can wreak in professional settings but also sparked the global #MeToo movement, illustrating how the exposure of such personalities can lead to broader social change.

In the realm of international relations, the leadership of North Korea's Kim Jong-un provides a stark example of how Dark Triad traits can shape a nation's policies. Kim's regime is characterized by a cult of personality reflective of extreme narcissism, Machiavellian tactics in diplomatic negotiations, and psychopathic disregard for the suffering of the North Korean people. The case of North Korea under Kim's leadership demonstrates how Dark Triad traits at the highest levels of government can lead to human rights abuses, international tensions, and the prioritization of personal power over national wellbeing.

These case studies across various domains illustrate the complex and often destructive impact of Dark Triad personalities in real-world contexts. While these traits can sometimes drive individuals to positions of power and influence, they frequently lead to negative outcomes for organizations, societies, and interpersonal relationships. Understanding how Dark Triad personalities operate in different settings is crucial for developing strategies to mitigate their harmful effects and for recognizing the warning signs in our personal and professional lives.

The real-world implications of Dark Triad personalities underscore the importance of fostering environments that value empathy, ethical behavior, and genuine collaboration. By promoting these positive traits and implementing systems that check unconstrained power, we can work towards minimizing the destructive influence of Dark Triad individuals in our societies, workplaces, and personal relationships.

Chapter 5: The Dark Triad in Relationships

Romantic Relationships

Romantic relationships involving individuals with Dark Triad traits are often characterized by a complex interplay of charm, deceit, and manipulation. These individuals possess a unique ability to attract partners through their charismatic and alluring personalities, often appearing confident, exciting, and irresistible. Their initial charm can be overwhelming, sweeping potential partners off their feet with grand gestures, intense attention, and seemingly genuine affection. This phase, often referred to as "love bombing," is a calculated strategy employed by Dark Triad individuals to quickly establish a strong emotional connection and create a sense of dependency in their partners.

The charm exhibited by Dark Triad individuals is not merely superficial; it is a finely honed skill that allows them to present themselves in the most appealing light possible. They are adept at reading social cues and adjusting their behavior to match their partner's desires and expectations.

This chameleon-like ability enables them to create an idealized version of themselves, one that perfectly aligns with their partner's fantasies and preferences. By doing so, they can rapidly form intense connections and foster a sense of intimacy that may feel unparalleled to their partners.

However, beneath the surface of this enchanting facade lies a web of deceit and manipulation. Dark Triad individuals are skilled in the art of deception, often crafting elaborate lies and half-truths to maintain their carefully constructed image. They may fabricate or exaggerate their accomplishments, experiences, or feelings to appear more desirable or to elicit sympathy and admiration from their partners. This deceptive behavior serves multiple purposes: it allows them to maintain control over the narrative of the relationship, shields them from vulnerability, and enables them to exploit their partners' trust and affection.

The manipulative tactics employed by Dark Triad individuals in romantic relationships are diverse and often subtle. They may use gaslighting techniques to make their partners doubt their own perceptions and memories, gradually eroding their self-confidence and independence. By creating confusion and uncertainty, they can more easily exert control over their partners' thoughts and behaviors. Additionally, they may employ emotional blackmail, using guilt, fear, or obligation to manipulate their partners into compliance with their wishes.

One of the primary goals of Dark Triad individuals in romantic relationships is to establish and maintain control over their partners. They achieve this through a combination of positive and negative reinforcement, alternating between lavish praise and affection and withholding emotional support or expressing disappointment. This inconsistent behavior creates a sense of emotional instability in their partners, who become increasingly dependent on the Dark Triad individual's approval and validation.

Dark Triad individuals often engage in strategic game-playing within their romantic relationships. They may intentionally provoke jealousy by flirting with others or mentioning past romantic interests, aiming to keep their partners insecure and constantly vying for their attention. They might also employ the "push-pull" technique, alternating between intense affection and cold detachment to keep their partners off-balance and emotionally invested in the relationship.

The sexual dynamics in relationships with Dark Triad individuals can be particularly complex. They often use sex as a tool for manipulation and control, employing their charm and allure to seduce partners and create a strong physical bond. However, they may also withhold sexual intimacy as a form of punishment or to maintain power over their partners. Dark Triad individuals might engage in infidelity, justifying their actions through their sense of entitlement or using it as a means to assert their independence and desirability.

It's important to note that not all Dark Triad individuals behave identically in romantic relationships. The specific manifestation of these traits can vary depending on which of the Dark Triad components (narcissism, Machiavellianism, or psychopathy) is most dominant in the individual. For instance, those high in narcissism may be more focused on maintaining an idealized image and seeking constant admiration from their partners. In contrast, those high in Machiavellianism might be more calculated in their approach, viewing the relationship as a strategic alliance to be leveraged for personal gain.

The long-term effects of being in a romantic relationship with a Dark Triad individual can be severe and lasting. Partners often experience a gradual erosion of their self-esteem, independence, and sense of reality. They may find themselves isolated from friends and family, as the Dark Triad individual seeks to monopolize their attention and limit outside influences. The constant emotional manipulation and deceit can lead to anxiety, depression, and even symptoms of post-traumatic stress disorder in some cases.

Despite the negative impacts, many partners of Dark Triad individuals find it challenging to leave the relationship. The intense emotional highs experienced during the initial stages of the relationship, combined with the intermittent reinforcement of affection and attention, can create a powerful psychological bond. Additionally, the Dark Triad individual's manipulative tactics often instill a sense of fear, obligation, or guilt in their partners, making it difficult for them to contemplate ending the relationship.

It's crucial to recognize that not all charming or confident individuals possess Dark Triad traits, and not all relationships with Dark Triad individuals follow the same pattern. However, understanding the potential dynamics and warning signs can be valuable for individuals navigating romantic relationships. Awareness of these patterns can help people protect themselves from manipulation and make informed decisions about their relationships.

For those who find themselves in relationships with Dark Triad individuals, seeking support from trusted friends, family members, or mental health professionals can be crucial. These support systems can provide perspective, validation, and assistance in recognizing and addressing the harmful dynamics within the relationship. Ultimately, while the allure of Dark Triad individuals can be powerful, it's essential for individuals to prioritize their own well-being and emotional health in romantic relationships.

Friendships and Family

The intricate web of relationships that Dark Triad individuals weave within their friendships and family circles is a complex and often troubling phenomenon. These individuals, characterized by their narcissistic, Machiavellian, and psychopathic traits, approach personal relationships with a unique set of motivations and behaviors that can profoundly impact those closest to them. Understanding the dynamics of these relationships is crucial for both those who may find themselves entangled with Dark Triad personalities and for professionals seeking to provide support and intervention.

At the core of Dark Triad individuals' approach to friendships and family relationships is their tendency to view others as tools for personal gain rather than as genuine emotional connections. This instrumental view of relationships stems from their inherent lack of empathy and their prioritization of self-interest above all else. In friendships, Dark Triad individuals may cultivate a wide network of acquaintances, presenting themselves as charismatic and likable. However, these relationships often lack depth and are maintained primarily for the benefits they can provide, such as social status, resources, or opportunities for manipulation.

Within family structures, Dark Triad individuals can create particularly toxic dynamics. Their need for admiration and control can lead to manipulative behaviors towards parents, siblings, and even their own children. They may engage in emotional blackmail, guilt-tripping, or gaslighting to maintain their position of power within the family unit. This behavior can result in long-lasting psychological damage to family members, who may struggle with self-esteem issues, trust problems, and difficulties in forming healthy relationships of their own.

The exploitation of trust is a hallmark of Dark Triad individuals in both friendships and family relationships. They excel at identifying others' vulnerabilities and using this knowledge to their advantage. In friendships, they may initially present themselves as highly supportive and understanding, encouraging others to confide in them. However, this information is often stored away to be used later for manipulation or blackmail. Within families, Dark Triad individuals may exploit the inherent trust and loyalty that family members typically share, taking advantage of financial resources, emotional support, or family connections without reciprocation.

One of the most insidious aspects of Dark Triad individuals in relationships is their ability to undermine trust gradually. They may engage in subtle forms of sabotage, such as spreading rumors or planting seeds of doubt about other relationships in the victim's life. This behavior serves to isolate the victim, making them more dependent on the Dark Triad individual and less likely to seek outside support or perspective. Over time, this erosion of trust can extend beyond the immediate relationship, causing the victim to question their judgment and ability to form healthy connections with others.

The impact of Dark Triad individuals on children within a family setting deserves particular attention. Children raised by parents with Dark Triad traits often experience a range of adverse effects, including emotional neglect, inconsistent parenting, and exposure to manipulative behaviors. These children may develop maladaptive coping mechanisms, struggle with attachment issues, and be at higher risk for developing mental health problems later in life. Additionally, they may internalize the toxic relationship patterns they observe, perpetuating the cycle in their own future relationships.

In friendships, Dark Triad individuals often create a façade of being the "perfect friend." They may go to great lengths to appear supportive, generous, and loyal on the surface. However, this behavior is typically motivated by a desire to create a sense of obligation in others, which can be exploited later. Friends of Dark Triad individuals may find themselves constantly indebted, either emotionally or materially, feeling pressured to reciprocate favors or support that was never genuinely offered in the first place.

The competitive nature of Dark Triad individuals can also manifest in their friendships and family relationships. They may view close relationships as a zero-sum game, where the success or happiness of others is perceived as a threat to their own status or well-being. This can lead to sabotaging behaviors, where they actively undermine the achievements or relationships of those close to them. In family settings, this might manifest as pitting siblings against each other or undermining a spouse's career ambitions.

Dark Triad individuals often employ a tactic known as "love bombing" in the early stages of friendships or romantic relationships. This involves showering the target with excessive affection, attention, and promises of a deep, meaningful connection. However, this intensity is not sustainable and is typically followed by a period of devaluation once the Dark Triad individual feels they have secured the other person's trust and attachment. This cycle of idealization and devaluation can be particularly confusing and damaging for those on the receiving end, leading to emotional instability and a distorted sense of self-worth.

The ability of Dark Triad individuals to compartmentalize their lives allows them to maintain multiple, often conflicting, relationships simultaneously. They may present different personas to different friends or family members, tailoring their behavior to maximize the benefits they can extract from each relationship. This chameleon-like quality makes it difficult for others to recognize the true nature of the Dark Triad individual, as they may hear conflicting accounts from different people in their life.

Recovery and healing for those who have been in close relationships with Dark Triad individuals can be a challenging process. The erosion of trust and self-esteem that occurs in these relationships often requires professional intervention to overcome. Victims may need to relearn healthy relationship patterns, establish firm boundaries, and work through feelings of guilt, shame, and self-doubt that have been instilled by the Dark Triad individual.

For mental health professionals and researchers, understanding the dynamics of Dark Triad individuals in friendships and family relationships is crucial for developing effective intervention strategies. This includes recognizing the subtle signs of manipulation and exploitation, as well as understanding the long-term psychological impact on victims. Developing support systems and educational programs to help individuals identify and protect themselves from Dark Triad behaviors in their personal relationships is an important area of focus.

Power Dynamics

Relationships involving individuals with Dark Triad traits are often characterized by significant power imbalances. These imbalances stem from the inherent manipulative and exploitative tendencies of narcissists, Machiavellians, and psychopaths. The power dynamics in such relationships are complex and multifaceted, with the Dark Triad individual typically seeking to establish and maintain control over their partner.

Narcissists, in particular, thrive on power and admiration. They often enter relationships with the primary goal of boosting their own ego and self-esteem. In these relationships, the narcissist may initially shower their partner with attention and affection, a technique known as "love bombing." This creates a sense of dependency and indebtedness in their partner, setting the stage for future manipulation. As the relationship progresses, the narcissist gradually shifts the power balance in their favor, demanding more attention and admiration while giving less in return.

The power imbalance in relationships with narcissists is further exacerbated by their tendency to use emotional manipulation tactics. They may employ gaslighting techniques, causing their partner to doubt their own perceptions and memories. This erosion of self-confidence makes the partner more susceptible to the narcissist's influence and control. Additionally, narcissists often use intermittent reinforcement, alternating between affection and coldness, to keep their partner off-balance and constantly seeking approval.

Machiavellian individuals, known for their strategic thinking and manipulative behaviors, approach relationships as a means to an end. They view their partners as resources to be exploited for personal gain. The power dynamics in these relationships are often subtle and insidious, with the Machiavellian partner gradually accumulating influence and control through calculated actions and decisions.

One common tactic employed by Machiavellians is information control. They may selectively share or withhold information to maintain an advantage over their partner. This creates an asymmetry of knowledge, leaving the partner feeling uninformed and dependent on the Machiavellian for crucial information. Additionally, Machiavellians excel at identifying and exploiting their partner's weaknesses and insecurities, using this knowledge to further tilt the power balance in their favor.

Machiavellians also tend to cultivate a network of allies and supporters within their social circle, often at the expense of their partner's relationships. This social maneuvering serves to isolate their partner and increase their dependence on the Machiavellian. By controlling the narrative and presenting a carefully crafted image to others, Machiavellians can effectively undermine their partner's credibility and support system.

Psychopathic individuals present perhaps the most extreme case of power imbalance in relationships. Their lack of empathy, combined with their impulsivity and thrill-seeking tendencies, often leads to highly volatile and potentially dangerous relationship dynamics. Psychopaths view their partners as objects to be used and discarded at will, with little regard for their emotional or physical well-being.

The power dynamics in relationships with psychopaths are often characterized by fear and intimidation. Psychopaths may use threats, both explicit and implicit, to control their partners. They may exploit their partner's fears and vulnerabilities, creating a constant state of anxiety and uncertainty. This emotional terrorism serves to keep the partner compliant and submissive, further cementing the psychopath's dominance in the relationship.

Psychopaths are also adept at creating financial dependence in their partners. They may encourage their partners to quit their jobs or take on debt, ostensibly for the benefit of the relationship. However, the true motive is to increase the partner's reliance on the psychopath, making it more difficult for them to leave the relationship. This financial control becomes yet another tool in the psychopath's arsenal for maintaining power and control.

It's important to note that the power imbalances in relationships with Dark Triad individuals are not always immediately apparent. These individuals often possess considerable charm and charisma, which they use to mask their true intentions. In the early stages of a relationship, they may present themselves as attentive, caring, and even submissive partners. This facade serves to lower their partner's defenses and create a false sense of security.

As the relationship progresses, the Dark Triad individual gradually asserts more control. They may use a combination of positive reinforcement (praise, gifts, affection) and negative reinforcement (withdrawal of affection, silent treatment, criticism) to shape their partner's behavior. This conditioning process slowly erodes the partner's autonomy and self-esteem, making them more susceptible to manipulation and control.

The power dynamics in these relationships are further complicated by the Dark Triad individual's ability to exploit societal norms and expectations. For example, they may use gender roles or cultural expectations to justify their controlling behavior. They might frame their actions as "protective" or "traditional," making it difficult for their partner to recognize or challenge the underlying power imbalance.

Another factor contributing to the power imbalance is the Dark Triad individual's lack of emotional investment in the relationship. While their partner may be deeply emotionally invested, the Dark Triad individual views the relationship primarily as a means to an end. This emotional asymmetry gives them a significant advantage, as they are willing to employ tactics that their partner would consider unthinkable, such as infidelity, deception, or emotional blackmail.

The cumulative effect of these power dynamics can be devastating for the partner of a Dark Triad individual. Over time, they may experience a loss of self-identity, decreased self-esteem, and a sense of helplessness. The constant manipulation and emotional abuse can lead to symptoms of anxiety, depression, and even post-traumatic stress disorder.

Recognizing and addressing these power imbalances is crucial for individuals involved in relationships with Dark Triad personalities. However, this can be extremely challenging due to the manipulative nature of these individuals. They often gaslight their partners, dismissing or minimizing their concerns and making them doubt their own perceptions.

Breaking free from these toxic power dynamics often requires external support and intervention. Friends, family, or professional therapists can provide the perspective and validation needed to recognize the unhealthy patterns in the relationship. They can also offer emotional support and practical assistance in establishing boundaries or leaving the relationship if necessary.

Understanding the power dynamics typical of relationships with Dark Triad individuals is essential not only for those directly involved but also for professionals working in fields such as psychology, counseling, and law enforcement. By recognizing these patterns, they can better assist victims and develop strategies to prevent and address the abuse of power in intimate relationships.

Breaking Free:

Recognizing a toxic relationship with a Dark Triad individual is the crucial first step toward breaking free. These relationships often begin intensely, with the Dark

Triad partner showering their target with attention, affection, and promises. This love bombing phase can be intoxicating, making it difficult to see the red flags that emerge later. As time passes, the Dark Triad individual's true nature begins to surface. They may become controlling, manipulative, or emotionally abusive. They might gaslight their partner, making them question their own perceptions and memories. The victim may find themselves walking on eggshells, constantly trying to appease their partner to avoid conflict or punishment.

Physical and emotional exhaustion are common symptoms of being in a relationship with a Dark Triad personality. Victims often report feeling drained, anxious, and depressed. They may lose interest in activities they once enjoyed or become isolated from friends and family. The Dark Triad partner may actively work to separate their victim from support systems, making them more dependent and easier to control. Financial abuse can also occur, with the Dark Triad individual taking control of finances or sabotaging their partner's career.

Recognizing these patterns is essential for victims to understand that they are in a toxic relationship. It's important to remember that the behavior of a Dark Triad partner is not the victim's fault, nor is it something they can change through love, patience, or understanding. The nature of Dark Triad personalities means that their harmful behaviors are deeply ingrained and unlikely to change without significant professional intervention — which many are unwilling to pursue.

Once a person recognizes they are in a toxic relationship with a Dark Triad individual, coping strategies become crucial. One important strategy is to maintain connections with trusted friends and family members, even if it must be done in secret. These support systems can provide emotional validation, practical assistance, and a reality check against the Dark Triad partner's manipulations. Keeping a private journal can also be helpful, allowing the victim to track patterns of behavior and maintain a clear record of events that the Dark Triad partner might later try to deny or distort.

Setting and maintaining boundaries is another vital coping strategy, although it can be challenging with a Dark Triad partner. This might involve refusing to engage in arguments, not responding to provocations, or limiting contact in certain situations. Learning about manipulation tactics and emotional abuse can help victims recognize when these strategies are being used against them, making it easier to resist their effects.

Self-care becomes particularly important when dealing with a Dark Triad partner. This can include maintaining physical health through exercise and proper nutrition, practicing stress-reduction techniques like meditation or yoga, and engaging in activities that bring joy and a sense of self-worth. Therapy can be an invaluable resource, providing a safe space to process emotions and develop coping strategies. However, it's crucial to find a therapist who understands the dynamics of toxic relationships and personality disorders.

While coping strategies can help manage the immediate challenges of being in a relationship with a Dark Triad individual, it's important to recognize that these relationships rarely improve over time. The most effective way to break free from a toxic relationship with a Dark Triad personality is to leave. However, this is often easier said than done. Dark Triad individuals can be extremely persuasive and may use a variety of tactics to prevent their partner from leaving, including threats, guilt-tripping, or promises to change.

Planning an exit strategy is crucial for safely leaving a relationship with a Dark Triad individual. This may involve secretly saving money, gathering important documents, and finding a safe place to stay. It's important to have a support system in place, whether that's friends, family, or a domestic violence organization. If there are children involved, their safety must be a top priority in any exit plan.

When leaving, it's essential to be prepared for the Dark Triad individual's reaction. They may initially try to win their partner back with grand gestures and promises. If this doesn't work, they might turn to threats, stalking, or other forms of harassment. Having a safety plan in place and being aware of legal options, such as restraining orders, can help protect against these behaviors.

After leaving a relationship with a Dark Triad personality, the recovery process begins. This can be a challenging time, as victims may struggle with a range of emotions including guilt, grief, anger, and fear. They may also need to rebuild their sense of self and learn to trust again. Therapy can be particularly beneficial during this stage, helping individuals process their experiences and develop healthy coping mechanisms.

Rebuilding self-esteem is a crucial part of recovery. Dark Triad individuals often systematically undermine their partner's confidence, and reversing this damage takes time and effort. Engaging in activities that bring a sense of accomplishment, surrounding oneself with supportive people, and practicing self-compassion can all contribute to rebuilding self-esteem.

Learning to recognize the warning signs of Dark Triad personalities can help prevent falling into similar relationships in the future. This doesn't mean becoming paranoid or distrustful, but rather developing a healthy sense of caution and learning to trust one's instincts. It's also important to work on any personal vulnerabilities that may have made one susceptible to a Dark Triad individual in the first place, such as codependency or low self-esteem.

Recovery is not a linear process, and there may be setbacks along the way. It's common for individuals to experience trauma bonding, where they feel a strong attachment to their abuser despite the harm they've experienced. This can lead to thoughts of returning to the relationship, especially during times of stress or loneliness. Having a strong support system and coping strategies in place can help resist these urges and stay committed to healing.

Breaking free from a toxic relationship with a Dark Triad personality is a challenging journey, but it's one that leads to freedom, self-discovery, and the possibility of healthier relationships in the future. By recognizing the signs of a toxic relationship, implementing coping strategies, planning a safe exit, and committing to the recovery process, individuals can break free from the destructive influence of Dark Triad personalities and reclaim their lives. While the process may be difficult, the reward is a life free from manipulation and abuse, and the opportunity to build genuine, mutually respectful relationships.

Chapter 6: Dark Triad in the Workplace

Corporate Psychopaths

Corporate psychopaths represent a particularly intriguing subset of Dark Triad individuals who have managed to navigate the complex landscape of the business world with remarkable success. These individuals, characterized by their lack of empathy, manipulative tendencies, and ruthless ambition, often rise to positions of power and influence within organizations. Their ability to charm, deceive, and exploit others for personal gain allows them to climb the corporate ladder swiftly, leaving a trail of destruction in their wake.

The concept of the "successful psychopath" challenges traditional notions of psychopathy as solely associated with criminal behavior. In the corporate setting, these individuals may not engage in overtly illegal activities but instead operate within the gray areas of ethical conduct. They excel at identifying and exploiting loopholes in company policies, manipulating financial reports, and bending rules to their advantage. Their charisma and superficial charm enable them to create a façade of competence and leadership, often fooling colleagues and superiors alike.

Corporate psychopaths are driven by an insatiable appetite for power, status, and material wealth. They view the workplace as a battlefield where they must dominate and conquer at any cost. This ruthless ambition manifests in various ways, such as taking credit for others' work, sabotaging colleagues' efforts, and engaging in office politics to advance their own agenda. They are masters of impression management, presenting themselves as indispensable assets to the organization while simultaneously undermining its long-term stability and success.

One of the most dangerous aspects of corporate psychopaths is their ability to create toxic work environments. Their lack of empathy and disregard for others' well-being leads to increased stress, decreased morale, and high turnover rates among employees. They often surround themselves with sycophants and yes-men, creating an echo chamber that reinforces their distorted worldview. This can result in a culture of fear and mistrust, where ethical concerns are dismissed, and whistleblowers are silenced or ostracized.

The impact of corporate psychopaths extends beyond the immediate workplace. Their actions can have far-reaching consequences for entire industries and even national economies. High-profile cases of corporate fraud and financial scandals often reveal the presence of psychopathic traits among key executives. These individuals' willingness to take extreme risks, coupled with their lack of concern for potential negative outcomes, can lead to catastrophic failures that affect countless lives.

Identifying corporate psychopaths can be challenging, as they are adept at concealing their true nature. They often possess a superficial understanding of social norms and can mimic appropriate emotional responses when necessary. However, careful observation may reveal telltale signs, such as a pattern of broken promises, inconsistent behavior, and a tendency to shift blame onto others. Their relationships tend to be shallow and transactional, with little genuine emotional connection to colleagues or subordinates.

The rise of corporate psychopaths to positions of power raises important questions about the values and priorities of modern business culture. The emphasis on short-term profits, aggressive competition, and individual achievement may inadvertently create an environment that rewards psychopathic traits. Organizations that prioritize charisma and confidence over empathy and ethical conduct may find themselves vulnerable to the destructive influence of these individuals.

Addressing the issue of corporate psychopaths requires a multifaceted approach. At the organizational level, companies must implement robust screening processes and background checks to identify potential red flags during the hiring process. Regular performance evaluations should include assessments of ethical conduct and interpersonal skills, not just financial metrics. Creating a culture that values collaboration, transparency, and ethical behavior can help mitigate the negative impact of psychopathic individuals.

Leadership development programs should focus on cultivating emotional intelligence, empathy, and ethical decision-making skills. By promoting these qualities, organizations can create a pipeline of leaders who are better equipped to recognize and counteract the influence of corporate psychopaths. Additionally, implementing strong governance structures and whistleblower protection policies can help expose and address unethical behavior before it escalates.

On a broader scale, there is a need for increased awareness and education about the presence of psychopathic traits in the corporate world. Business schools and professional development programs should incorporate discussions of ethics, corporate social responsibility, and the potential dangers of unchecked ambition. By fostering a more nuanced understanding of leadership and success, we can begin to shift away from the glorification of ruthless, win-at-all-costs mentalities.

The legal and regulatory landscape also plays a crucial role in addressing the issue of corporate psychopaths. Stricter enforcement of existing laws, coupled with the development of new regulations to address emerging ethical challenges, can help create a more hostile environment for those who seek to exploit others for personal gain. Increased accountability for executives and board members can serve as a deterrent to psychopathic behavior and encourage more responsible corporate governance.

It is important to note that not all successful business leaders exhibit psychopathic traits, and not all individuals with psychopathic tendencies rise to positions of power. The corporate world is complex and multifaceted, with many factors contributing to an individual's success or failure. However, the presence of corporate psychopaths represents a significant challenge that must be addressed to create healthier, more sustainable business practices.

As research in this field continues to evolve, new insights and strategies for managing corporate psychopaths are likely to emerge. Interdisciplinary approaches that combine psychology, organizational behavior, and business ethics may yield more effective methods for identifying and mitigating the risks associated with these individuals. By remaining vigilant and committed to promoting ethical leadership, organizations can work towards creating environments that are less hospitable to the destructive influence of corporate psychopaths.

The phenomenon of corporate psychopaths serves as a stark reminder of the darker aspects of human nature and the potential for individuals to exploit systems for personal gain. By acknowledging and addressing this issue, we can work towards creating more equitable, ethical, and sustainable business practices that benefit not just a select few, but society as a whole. The challenge lies in balancing the drive for success and innovation with the need for compassion, integrity, and social responsibility in the corporate world.

Toxic Work Environments

Toxic work environments are breeding grounds for the Dark Triad traits of narcissism, Machiavellianism, and psychopathy. These personality characteristics can create a workplace culture where manipulation, backstabbing, and unethical behavior become the norm rather than the exception. When individuals with these traits occupy positions of power or influence within an organization, their destructive behaviors can permeate throughout the entire company, leading to a toxic atmosphere that affects employee morale, productivity, and overall well-being.

Narcissism plays a significant role in fostering toxic work environments. Narcissistic individuals are driven by an insatiable need for admiration and recognition, often at the expense of others. In the workplace, this manifests as a constant need to be the center of attention, taking credit for others' work, and belittling colleagues to maintain their perceived superiority. Narcissistic leaders may create a culture of favoritism, where employees who feed their ego are rewarded, while those who challenge or question them are marginalized or punished. This dynamic can lead to a breakdown in teamwork and collaboration, as employees become more focused on pleasing the narcissistic leader than on achieving organizational goals.

The presence of narcissistic individuals in the workplace can also contribute to a culture of excessive competition and cutthroat behavior. As narcissists are primarily concerned with their own success and image, they may engage in sabotage or undermining of their colleagues' efforts to maintain their position at the top. This behavior can create an atmosphere of distrust and paranoia, where employees are constantly on guard against potential threats to their job security or status within the organization. The resulting stress and anxiety can lead to decreased job satisfaction, increased burnout, and higher turnover rates.

Machiavellianism, another component of the Dark Triad, further exacerbates toxic work environments through its emphasis on manipulation and strategic thinking. Machiavellian individuals are skilled at identifying and exploiting others' weaknesses for personal gain. In the workplace, this can manifest as spreading rumors, engaging in office politics, and using deceit to advance their own agendas. Machiavellian employees may form alliances with colleagues solely for the purpose of gaining information or leverage, only to discard these relationships when they are no longer useful.

The presence of Machiavellian traits in leadership positions can lead to a culture of mistrust and secrecy within the organization. Leaders who exhibit these characteristics may withhold important information from their subordinates, play employees against each other, or use manipulation tactics to maintain control. This lack of transparency and honesty can create an environment where employees feel constantly on edge, unsure of where they stand or who they can trust. As a result, communication breakdowns become common, and valuable information may be withheld or distorted, hindering the organization's ability to function effectively.

Psychopathy, the third component of the Dark Triad, introduces a level of callousness and lack of empathy that can be particularly damaging in the workplace. Psychopathic individuals are characterized by their ability to charm and manipulate others while lacking genuine emotional connections or concern for their well-being. In a work setting, psychopathic traits can manifest as a disregard for ethical considerations, a willingness to take risks at the expense of others, and a tendency to exploit colleagues for personal gain.

Psychopathic leaders may create a culture of fear and intimidation, using threats and coercion to maintain control over their subordinates. They may push employees to engage in unethical or illegal activities to achieve business goals, disregarding the potential consequences for individuals or the organization as a whole. This disregard for ethics and morality can lead to a breakdown in corporate values and integrity, potentially resulting in legal issues, reputational damage, and financial losses for the company.

The combination of narcissism, Machiavellianism, and psychopathy in the workplace can create a perfect storm of toxic behavior. Employees may find themselves caught in a web of manipulation, where they are forced to navigate complex social dynamics and power struggles just to perform their job duties. This constant state of vigilance and stress can lead to decreased job satisfaction, increased absenteeism, and higher rates of mental health issues among employees.

In toxic work environments influenced by Dark Triad traits, employees may feel pressured to adopt similar behaviors to survive or advance within the organization. This can create a cycle of toxicity, where unethical and manipulative behaviors become normalized and even rewarded. As a result, individuals who prioritize integrity and ethical conduct may find themselves at a disadvantage, leading to a talent drain as high-quality employees seek opportunities elsewhere.

The impact of toxic work environments extends beyond the immediate workplace, affecting employees' personal lives and overall well-being. The stress and negativity experienced at work can spill over into personal relationships, leading to increased conflict and decreased life satisfaction. Additionally, the constant exposure to manipulative and unethical behavior can erode an individual's own moral compass, potentially leading to long-term changes in their values and behavior.

Organizations that allow toxic work environments to flourish may experience significant negative consequences. Employee turnover rates tend to be higher in toxic workplaces, leading to increased recruitment and training costs. Productivity and innovation may suffer as employees become disengaged and focused on self-preservation rather than contributing to the company's success. Furthermore, the reputation of the organization may be damaged, making it difficult to attract top talent and potentially impacting customer relationships and business partnerships.

Addressing toxic work environments influenced by Dark Triad traits requires a multifaceted approach. Organizations must prioritize creating a culture of transparency, accountability, and ethical behavior from the top down. This includes implementing robust hiring and promotion processes that screen for Dark Triad traits and prioritize emotional intelligence and ethical leadership. Regular employee feedback mechanisms and 360-degree evaluations can help identify problematic behaviors and allow for early intervention.

Training programs that focus on emotional intelligence, conflict resolution, and ethical decision-making can help employees develop the skills needed to navigate complex workplace dynamics and resist manipulation. Additionally, establishing clear policies and procedures for reporting unethical behavior and protecting whistleblowers can create a safer environment for employees to speak up against toxic practices.

Leadership plays a crucial role in combating toxic work environments. Leaders must model ethical behavior, promote open communication, and foster a culture of trust and collaboration. By recognizing and rewarding positive behaviors while addressing toxic ones promptly and consistently, leaders can set the tone for a healthier workplace culture.

Leadership and Control

The Dark Triad can significantly influence leadership styles in the workplace, often resulting in authoritarian, exploitative, and corrupt leadership practices. Leaders who possess these traits tend to prioritize their own interests and power over the well-being of their subordinates and the organization as a whole. This subpoint will explore how Dark Triad traits manifest in leadership roles and the impact they have on organizational culture, employee morale, and overall business performance.

Narcissistic leaders are characterized by their grandiose sense of self-importance, need for admiration, and lack of empathy. In leadership positions, these individuals often create a cult of personality around themselves, demanding unwavering loyalty and praise from their subordinates. They may take credit for others' achievements and dismiss or belittle ideas that do not align with their own. Narcissistic leaders frequently engage in self-promotion, using their position to boost their ego and maintain a facade of superiority. This behavior can lead to a toxic work environment where employees feel undervalued and afraid to voice their opinions or concerns.

Machiavellian leaders, on the other hand, are master manipulators who prioritize power and control above all else. They excel at strategic thinking and are willing to use deception and manipulation to achieve their goals. In leadership roles, Machiavellian individuals often create complex webs of alliances and rivalries within the organization, pitting employees against each other to maintain their own position of power. They may engage in unethical practices, such as withholding information or spreading rumors, to advance their agenda. This leadership style can result in a culture of mistrust and paranoia, where employees are constantly on guard and struggle to collaborate effectively.

Psychopathic leaders are perhaps the most dangerous of the Dark Triad, as they lack empathy and remorse while possessing a high degree of charm and charisma. These individuals often rise to positions of power through their ability to manipulate others and their willingness to take risks. In leadership roles, psychopathic individuals may engage in reckless decision-making, disregarding the potential consequences for their employees or the organization. They may also exhibit callousness towards their subordinates, viewing them as expendable resources rather than valuable team members. This leadership style can lead to a culture of fear and instability, where employees are constantly on edge and afraid of becoming the next target of their leader's unpredictable behavior.

The combination of these Dark Triad traits in leadership positions often results in authoritarian management styles. Leaders with these characteristics tend to centralize power and decision-making, leaving little room for employee input or autonomy. They may implement strict hierarchies and rigid rules, enforcing compliance through fear and intimidation rather than trust and respect. This authoritarian approach can stifle creativity and innovation within the organization, as employees become hesitant to take risks or propose new ideas for fear of retribution.

Exploitative leadership is another common manifestation of Dark Triad traits in the workplace. Leaders with these characteristics often view their subordinates as tools to be used for personal gain rather than as individuals with their own needs and aspirations. They may overwork and underpay their employees, taking advantage of their labor while offering little in return. Exploitative leaders may also engage in favoritism, rewarding those who show unwavering loyalty while punishing or marginalizing those who dare to question their authority. This approach can lead to high turnover rates, low employee morale, and decreased productivity as workers become disillusioned and disengaged.

Corrupt leadership is a natural extension of the Dark Triad traits, as individuals with these characteristics often prioritize their own interests over ethical considerations. Leaders with high levels of narcissism, Machiavellianism, and psychopathy may engage in various forms of corruption, including embezzlement, fraud, and bribery. They may use their position of power to manipulate financial records, secure personal favors, or cover up misconduct. This corrupt behavior not only damages the organization's reputation and financial stability but also erodes trust within the workplace and broader community.

The impact of Dark Triad leadership on organizational culture cannot be overstated. These toxic leadership styles create an environment of fear, mistrust, and instability that permeates all levels of the organization. Employees working under such leaders often experience high levels of stress, anxiety, and burnout. They may become disengaged from their work, leading to decreased productivity and innovation. In extreme cases, the toxic culture created by Dark Triad leaders can result in widespread unethical behavior as employees adopt similar tactics to survive or advance within the organization.

The effects of Dark Triad leadership extend beyond the immediate workplace environment. Organizations led by individuals with these traits may engage in unethical business practices that harm customers, stakeholders, and the broader community. For example, a narcissistic leader might prioritize short-term profits over long-term sustainability, leading to environmental damage or product safety issues. A Machiavellian leader might engage in anti-competitive practices or manipulate market conditions to gain an unfair advantage. A psychopathic leader might disregard safety regulations or employee welfare in pursuit of personal gain.

Identifying and addressing Dark Triad traits in leadership positions is crucial for maintaining a healthy and productive workplace. Organizations should implement robust screening processes during hiring and promotion decisions to identify individuals with these characteristics. This may include personality assessments, thorough background checks, and in-depth interviews with references. Additionally, companies should establish clear ethical guidelines and accountability measures to prevent the abuse of power by those in leadership positions.

Developing a strong organizational culture that values transparency, collaboration, and ethical behavior can help counteract the negative effects of Dark Triad leadership. This includes fostering open communication channels, encouraging employee feedback, and promoting a sense of shared purpose and values. Organizations should also invest in leadership development programs that emphasize emotional intelligence, empathy, and ethical decision-making.

Addressing Dark Triad traits in leadership requires a multi-faceted approach that involves not only the organization but also employees, stakeholders, and regulatory bodies. By raising awareness of these toxic leadership styles and their detrimental effects, we can work towards creating more positive, productive, and ethical workplace environments. Ultimately, the goal is to cultivate leadership that prioritizes the well-being of employees, the success of the organization, and the broader social good over personal gain and power.

Surviving a Dark Triad Boss:

Working under or alongside a Dark Triad personality can be one of the most challenging experiences in one's professional life. These individuals, characterized by Machiavellianism, narcissism, and psychopathy, can create a toxic work environment that drains energy, stifles creativity, and undermines team morale. However, with the right strategies and mindset, it is possible to navigate this treacherous terrain and protect your career and well-being.

The first step in surviving a Dark Triad boss is to recognize the signs. Machiavellian bosses are master manipulators who prioritize their own interests above all else. They may use charm and flattery to get what they want, but they're also quick to exploit others' weaknesses. Narcissistic bosses have an inflated sense of self-importance and crave constant admiration. They may take credit for others' work and react poorly to criticism. Psychopathic bosses lack empathy and may engage in risky or unethical behavior without remorse. They can be charming on the surface but are often callous and unpredictable.

Once you've identified that you're dealing with a Dark Triad boss, it's crucial to maintain emotional distance. These individuals are skilled at manipulating emotions, so it's important not to take their behavior personally. Remember that their actions are a reflection of their own personality traits and not a judgment of your worth or abilities. Practice emotional detachment by focusing on facts and outcomes rather than getting caught up in the drama they create.

Documentation is your best friend when dealing with a Dark Triad boss. Keep detailed records of all interactions, assignments, and accomplishments. This includes saving emails, noting down verbal instructions, and documenting your contributions to projects. This paper trail can protect you from gaslighting attempts and provide evidence if you need to escalate issues to HR or upper management.

Setting clear boundaries is essential when working with Dark Triad personalities. Be firm and professional in your communications, and don't hesitate to assert yourself when necessary. Avoid sharing personal information that could be used against you, and maintain a professional demeanor at all times. If your boss makes unreasonable demands or crosses ethical lines, politely but firmly express your concerns and suggest alternatives.

Building a strong network within your organization can provide crucial support when dealing with a Dark Triad boss. Cultivate relationships with colleagues, other managers, and even clients or vendors. These connections can offer alternative perspectives, provide emotional support, and potentially serve as allies if conflicts arise. However, be cautious about openly criticizing your boss to others, as this could backfire if word gets back to them.

Developing a thick skin is crucial for survival in this environment. Dark Triad bosses often use criticism, belittlement, and emotional manipulation as tools of control. Learn to distinguish between constructive feedback and toxic behavior. When faced with unfair criticism, respond calmly and professionally, focusing on facts and solutions rather than getting defensive. Remember that their attacks are often more about their own insecurities than your performance.

Mastering the art of strategic agreement can be a valuable skill when dealing with a Dark Triad boss. This doesn't mean blindly agreeing with everything they say, but rather choosing your battles wisely. When possible, find ways to align your goals with theirs, presenting ideas in a way that appeals to their self-interest. Use phrases like "I agree with your point about X, and I think we could achieve even better results if we also consider Y."

Self-care is paramount when working in a stressful environment created by a Dark Triad boss. Make sure to prioritize your physical and mental health. Engage in regular exercise, practice stress-reduction techniques like meditation or yoga, and maintain a strong support system outside of work. Consider seeking professional help, such as counseling or therapy, to process your experiences and develop coping strategies.

Staying focused on your own goals and career development is crucial. Don't let the toxic environment derail your professional growth. Continue to seek out learning opportunities, take on challenging projects, and build your skills. This not only helps maintain your motivation but also makes you more marketable if you decide to seek opportunities elsewhere.

In some cases, the best strategy for dealing with a Dark Triad boss may be to plan your exit. If the situation is severely impacting your well-being and career prospects, and there's no sign of improvement, it may be time to explore other opportunities. Start discreetly networking and job searching while still maintaining your performance at your current position.

When interacting with a Dark Triad boss, it's important to manage your expectations. These individuals are unlikely to change their fundamental personality traits, so don't expect sudden transformations or moments of empathy. Instead, focus on managing the relationship in a way that protects your interests and allows you to perform your job effectively.

Learning to read your boss's moods and triggers can help you navigate daily interactions more smoothly. Pay attention to patterns in their behavior and try to anticipate potential conflicts. If you notice they're particularly stressed or agitated, it might be best to delay non-urgent matters or approach them more cautiously.

Developing a personal brand of competence and reliability can provide some protection against a Dark Triad boss's manipulations. Consistently deliver high-quality work, meet deadlines, and be known for your professionalism. This makes it harder for them to undermine you and can increase your value to the organization as a whole.

When communicating with a Dark Triad boss, be clear, concise, and confident. Present information in a way that appeals to their ego and self-interest. For example, when proposing a new idea, emphasize how it will make them look good or benefit the company's bottom line. Be prepared to back up your statements with data and facts.

Remember that knowledge is power when dealing with Dark Triad personalities. Educate yourself about their traits and tactics. Understanding the psychology behind their behavior can help you anticipate their moves and respond more effectively. Consider reading books or attending workshops on dealing with difficult personalities in the workplace.

Chapter 7: The Dark Triad and Crime

Criminal Behavior and the Dark Triad

The Dark Triad traits have long been associated with various forms of criminal behavior. This connection stems from the inherent characteristics of these personality traits, which often predispose individuals to engage in antisocial and illegal activities. The relationship between the Dark Triad and criminal behavior is complex and multifaceted, spanning a wide range of offenses from white-collar crimes to violent acts.

Machiavellianism, characterized by manipulation, cynicism, and pragmatic morality, is often linked to crimes involving deception and fraud. Individuals high in Machiavellianism tend to view others as mere tools for personal gain, making them more likely to engage in white-collar crimes such as embezzlement, insider trading, and corporate fraud. Their strategic thinking and ability to manipulate others allow them to orchestrate complex schemes, often evading detection for extended periods. These individuals may also be drawn to political corruption, using their cunning to exploit positions of power for personal benefit.

Narcissism, with its hallmarks of grandiosity, entitlement, and lack of empathy, contributes to criminal behavior in various ways. Narcissistic individuals may engage in crimes to maintain their inflated self-image or to seek admiration and attention. This can manifest in attention-seeking criminal acts, such as high-profile thefts or elaborate cons. Their sense of entitlement may lead them to believe they are above the law, resulting in a disregard for legal and ethical boundaries. White-collar crimes committed by narcissists often involve embezzlement or fraud, as they seek to accumulate wealth and status to fuel their grandiose self-image.

Psychopathy, perhaps the most notorious of the Dark Triad traits, is strongly associated with criminal behavior across the spectrum. Characterized by callousness, impulsivity, and lack of remorse, psychopathic individuals are more likely to engage in violent crimes, including assault, murder, and sexual offenses. Their lack of empathy and disregard for social norms make them particularly dangerous in criminal contexts. However, psychopathy is not limited to violent crime; many psychopaths excel in corporate settings, using their charm and ruthlessness to climb the ladder and commit white-collar offenses.

The interplay between these Dark Triad traits often exacerbates criminal tendencies. For instance, an individual high in both narcissism and psychopathy may be more likely to commit violent crimes for attention or to assert dominance. Similarly, a person with high levels of Machiavellianism and narcissism might be particularly adept at orchestrating elaborate financial frauds, combining manipulative skills with an insatiable desire for wealth and status.

In white-collar crime, the Dark Triad traits often manifest in sophisticated and far-reaching offenses. Corporate fraud, for example, may be perpetrated by individuals high in Machiavellianism who can navigate complex financial systems and manipulate others into complicity. Their ability to present a facade of trustworthiness while harboring ulterior motives makes them particularly dangerous in business settings. Narcissistic traits may drive executives to engage in insider trading or cook the books to maintain the appearance of success, while psychopathic traits can lead to a complete disregard for the consequences of their actions on employees, shareholders, and the broader economy.

The relationship between the Dark Triad and cybercrime is an area of growing concern. The anonymous nature of the internet provides a perfect playground for individuals high in Dark Triad traits to exploit others. Machiavellianism may manifest in elaborate phishing schemes or social engineering attacks, while narcissism could drive individuals to engage in attention-seeking hacks or cyber vandalism. Psychopathic traits might lead to more malicious forms of cybercrime, such as stalking, blackmail, or the distribution of harmful content.

Violent crimes committed by individuals high in Dark Triad traits often exhibit distinct patterns. Psychopathic offenders may engage in predatory violence, carefully planning their attacks and showing little emotional arousal during the act. Their lack of empathy allows them to inflict harm without remorse, often leading to serial offenses. Narcissistic individuals might resort to violence when their inflated self-image is threatened, resulting in crimes of passion or revenge. Machiavellian traits, while less directly associated with violence, may contribute to organized crime activities where violence is used as a tool for control and intimidation.

Sexual offenses are another area where Dark Triad traits play a significant role. Psychopathy, in particular, is strongly associated with sexual aggression and predatory behavior. The lack of empathy and callousness characteristic of psychopathy can lead to a complete disregard for the victim's consent or wellbeing. Narcissistic traits may contribute to sexual offenses through a sense of entitlement and a belief that others exist merely for their gratification. Machiavellianism, while not as directly linked to sexual offenses, may manifest in the manipulation and grooming of potential victims.

The Dark Triad's influence extends beyond individual criminal acts to broader criminal enterprises. Organized crime groups, for instance, may be led by individuals high in psychopathy who can maintain control through fear and intimidation. Their organizations might be structured and operated by those high in Machiavellianism, who excel at strategic planning and manipulation. Narcissistic traits among members could drive competition within the group and fuel the pursuit of power and status through criminal means.

Understanding the connection between Dark Triad traits and criminal behavior has significant implications for law enforcement and criminal justice systems. Recognizing the psychological profiles associated with different types of crimes can aid in investigation techniques, risk assessment, and rehabilitation strategies. For example, knowing that white-collar criminals often score high in Machiavellianism and narcissism can inform forensic accounting practices and corporate governance policies.

Prevention and intervention strategies must also consider the role of Dark Triad traits in criminal behavior. Early identification of these traits in individuals, particularly in adolescents, could allow for targeted interventions to mitigate the risk of future criminal activity.

This might involve specialized counseling, empathy training, or programs designed to channel dark traits into more prosocial outlets.

The legal system's approach to offenders with Dark Triad traits is another area of consideration. Traditional punitive measures may be less effective for individuals high in psychopathy, who are often resistant to behavior change and may view incarceration as an opportunity to hone their criminal skills. Alternative approaches, such as intensive supervision or specialized treatment programs, may be necessary to address the unique challenges posed by Dark Triad offenders.

Research into the neurobiological basis of Dark Triad traits and their relationship to criminal behavior is ongoing. Studies have identified differences in brain structure and function associated with these traits, particularly in areas related to empathy, impulse control, and moral decision-making. This research may eventually lead to new approaches in both prevention and rehabilitation, potentially including targeted neurological interventions.

The Dark Triad's influence on criminal behavior is a complex and evolving field of study. As our understanding of these personality traits and their manifestations in criminal contexts grows, so too does our ability to address the challenges they pose to society. By recognizing the unique risks associated with Dark Triad traits, we can develop more effective strategies for prevention, intervention, and rehabilitation, ultimately working towards a safer and more just society.

The Psychopath as a Criminal

Psychopathy and criminal behavior, particularly violent and antisocial acts have a lot in common. This connection is not merely anecdotal; extensive research has consistently demonstrated a strong correlation between psychopathic traits and criminal activities. While it is crucial to note that not all psychopaths engage in criminal behavior, and not all criminals are psychopaths, the link between psychopathy and crime is significant enough to warrant careful examination.

The hallmark traits of psychopathy, including lack of empathy, callousness, and impulsivity, create a perfect storm for potential criminal behavior. Psychopaths often view others as objects to be manipulated or exploited, rather than as fellow human beings with inherent worth. This emotional detachment allows them to commit acts that most people would find unthinkable, without experiencing guilt or remorse. Their impulsivity and thrill-seeking tendencies further increase the likelihood of engaging in risky or illegal activities.

One of the most chilling manifestations of psychopathy in the criminal world is the phenomenon of serial killers. While not all serial killers are psychopaths, and not all psychopaths become serial killers, there is a significant overlap between these two categories. Many of history's most notorious serial killers, such as Ted Bundy, John Wayne Gacy, and Jeffrey Dahmer, have displayed clear psychopathic traits. These individuals often exhibit a complete lack of empathy for their victims, coupled with a grandiose sense of self and a need for stimulation that drives them to commit repeated acts of violence.

The connection between psychopathy and serial killing is not coincidental. The emotional coldness and lack of empathy characteristic of psychopathy enable these individuals to commit heinous acts without experiencing the normal human reactions of guilt or horror. Moreover, their charm and manipulative abilities often allow them to lure victims and evade detection for extended periods. The thrill-seeking aspect of psychopathy may also play a role, as some serial killers report experiencing a "high" from their crimes, which drives them to repeat their actions.

Beyond serial killers, psychopathy is also strongly associated with repeat offenders in various criminal categories. Studies have shown that individuals with high levels of psychopathic traits are more likely to reoffend after release from prison compared to non-psychopathic offenders. This recidivism is partly due to the psychopath's inability to learn from past experiences or to be deterred by punishment. Their lack of concern for social norms and legal consequences, combined with their impulsivity, creates a pattern of persistent criminal behavior that is difficult to break.

The types of crimes committed by psychopaths often involve violence or exploitation of others. While they may engage in a wide range of criminal activities, including fraud, theft, and drug trafficking, psychopaths are particularly overrepresented in violent crime statistics. Their lack of empathy and callousness make them more prone to using violence as a means to an end, whether that end is personal gratification, financial gain, or the simple assertion of power over others.

It is important to note that psychopathy manifests differently in different individuals, and not all psychopaths will engage in overtly violent behavior. Some may channel their psychopathic traits into more socially acceptable, albeit still potentially harmful, pursuits. These individuals, often referred to as "successful psychopaths," may rise to positions of power in business, politics, or other fields, using their charm and manipulative abilities to advance their own interests at the expense of others.

The relationship between psychopathy and crime poses significant challenges for the criminal justice system. Traditional methods of rehabilitation and deterrence often prove ineffective for psychopathic offenders due to their lack of emotional responsiveness and inability to learn from punishment. This has led to debates about how best to manage psychopathic criminals within the justice system, with some arguing for longer sentences or specialized treatment programs.

Research into the neurobiological basis of psychopathy has provided some insights into why these individuals are prone to criminal behavior. Brain imaging studies have revealed differences in the structure and function of certain brain regions in psychopaths, particularly areas associated with emotion processing, impulse control, and moral decision-making. These biological differences may contribute to the psychopath's propensity for antisocial and criminal behavior, although the exact mechanisms are still not fully understood.

The early identification of psychopathic traits has become an area of interest for researchers and law enforcement alike. Some experts argue that early intervention might help prevent the development of criminal behavior in individuals with psychopathic tendencies. However, this approach raises ethical concerns about labeling and potentially stigmatizing individuals, especially young people, based on personality traits.

Understanding the link between psychopathy and crime is crucial not only for law enforcement and the criminal justice system but also for society as a whole. It highlights the need for more effective methods of prevention, intervention, and rehabilitation tailored to the unique characteristics of psychopathic offenders. At the same time, it underscores the importance of recognizing that psychopathy is a complex condition, and not all individuals with psychopathic traits will become criminals.

The study of psychopathy in the context of criminal behavior continues to evolve, with new research shedding light on the intricate relationships between personality, biology, environment, and criminal actions. As our understanding deepens, it may lead to more effective strategies for preventing and addressing psychopathy-related crime, ultimately contributing to safer communities and a more just society.

While the connection between psychopathy and crime, particularly violent crime, is well-established, it is essential to approach this topic with nuance. Psychopathy is just one of many factors that can contribute to criminal behavior, and many individuals with psychopathic traits never engage in illegal activities. By continuing to study and understand the complex interplay between psychopathy and crime, we can work towards more effective prevention and intervention strategies, while also challenging simplistic notions about the nature of criminality and mental health.

White-Collar Crime

White-collar crime represents a significant threat to society, often causing far-reaching economic and social consequences. While not as visibly violent as other forms of criminal activity, these financial and corporate transgressions can devastate individuals, businesses, and entire communities. The Dark Triad traits, particularly Machiavellianism and psychopathy, play a crucial role in understanding the motivations and methods behind white-collar crime.

Machiavellianism, characterized by manipulation, cynicism, and pragmatic morality, is particularly relevant in the context of white-collar crime. Individuals high in Machiavellianism are adept at strategic thinking and planning, often viewing others as mere pawns in their grand schemes. In the corporate world, this trait can manifest as a willingness to engage in unethical practices for personal gain or corporate advantage. Machiavellian executives may orchestrate elaborate fraud schemes, manipulate financial statements, or engage in insider trading without remorse.

These individuals excel at identifying and exploiting loopholes in financial systems and corporate governance structures. Their ability to charm and persuade others often allows them to rise to positions of power within organizations, where they can exert influence over decision-making processes and internal controls. Machiavellian white-collar criminals may cultivate a network of complicit colleagues, using their interpersonal skills to create alliances that facilitate their fraudulent activities.

Psychopathy, another component of the Dark Triad, also plays a significant role in white-collar crime. While often associated with violent offenses, psychopathy in the corporate world manifests as a lack of empathy, impulsivity, and a disregard for rules and social norms. Psychopathic traits can drive individuals to engage in high-risk financial behaviors, embezzlement, or large-scale fraud without considering the consequences for others.

The lack of empathy characteristic of psychopathy enables white-collar criminals to commit financial crimes without feeling guilt or remorse for their victims. This emotional detachment allows them to rationalize their actions, often viewing their crimes as victimless or even justified. Psychopathic individuals in corporate settings may exhibit a sense of entitlement, believing that rules do not apply to them and that they deserve whatever they can take, regardless of the means.

The combination of Machiavellianism and psychopathy can create a particularly dangerous profile in the realm of white-collar crime. These individuals possess the strategic thinking and manipulative skills of the

Machiavellian, coupled with the fearlessness and lack of empathy of the psychopath. This combination allows them to devise and execute complex fraudulent schemes while remaining untroubled by the ethical implications or potential consequences of their actions.

In the corporate environment, individuals with these Dark Triad traits may engage in various forms of financial misconduct. Accounting fraud, for instance, involves manipulating financial statements to mislead investors, regulators, or other stakeholders. A Machiavellian-psychopathic executive might orchestrate such a scheme, using their strategic thinking to identify ways to falsify records and their lack of empathy to disregard the potential harm to shareholders and employees.

Insider trading is another area where these traits can manifest. The ability to manipulate and exploit relationships, combined with a disregard for rules, may lead individuals to illegally trade on non-public information. Their charm and persuasive abilities might be used to gather sensitive information from unsuspecting colleagues, while their lack of concern for others allows them to profit at the expense of fair market practices.

Ponzi schemes and other investment frauds also bear the hallmarks of Dark Triad influence. The Machiavellian aspect comes into play in the careful construction of the scheme, creating an illusion of legitimacy and using social manipulation to attract investors. The psychopathic traits enable the perpetrator to continue the fraud over extended periods, showing no remorse as they deceive more victims and cause increasing financial harm.

Corporate espionage and theft of trade secrets represent another arena where Machiavellianism and psychopathy can intersect in white-collar crime. The strategic planning and manipulation associated with Machiavellianism may be employed to gain access to confidential information, while the risk-taking and rule-breaking tendencies of psychopathy drive the individual to act on this access without regard for legal or ethical boundaries.

It's important to note that the presence of Dark Triad traits does not inevitably lead to criminal behavior. Many individuals with these characteristics may operate within legal boundaries, although they may still engage in unethical practices that fall short of criminality. The corporate environment itself can sometimes enable or even reward certain Dark Triad behaviors, creating a culture that inadvertently fosters white-collar crime.

The impact of white-collar crime extends far beyond immediate financial losses. It erodes trust in financial institutions, damages the reputation of businesses, and can lead to job losses and economic instability. The presence of Dark Triad traits in perpetrators of these crimes often means that the harmful behavior continues until external forces intervene, as these individuals are unlikely to be deterred by moral considerations or potential consequences to others.

Addressing white-collar crime requires a multifaceted approach that takes into account the role of Dark Triad traits. Enhanced corporate governance structures, robust internal controls, and thorough background checks can help identify and mitigate risks associated with individuals high in Machiavellianism and psychopathy. Training programs that focus on ethical decision-making and creating a culture of integrity can also play a crucial role in preventing white-collar crime.

Law enforcement and regulatory bodies must also adapt their strategies to effectively combat white-collar crime influenced by Dark Triad traits. This may involve developing more sophisticated methods for detecting financial fraud, improving cooperation between different agencies, and implementing stricter penalties that serve as a deterrent even to those who lack empathy or concern for others.

Understanding the role of Machiavellianism and psychopathy in white-collar crime provides valuable insights for prevention and detection efforts. By recognizing the unique challenges posed by individuals with these traits, organizations and society as a whole can work towards creating more resilient systems that protect against financial exploitation and corporate fraud. While the Dark Triad presents significant risks in the corporate world, awareness and proactive measures can help mitigate their harmful effects and promote a more ethical business environment.

Case Studies

Ted Bundy stands out as one of the most notorious serial killers in American history, and his case provides a chilling example of Dark Triad traits manifesting in extreme criminal behavior. Bundy exhibited clear signs of narcissism, Machiavellianism, and psychopathy throughout his life and crimes. His narcissism was evident in his grandiose sense of self-importance and need for admiration. He cultivated a charismatic, likable public persona and was known for his good looks and charm. This allowed him to manipulate victims and evade suspicion. His Machiavellian tendencies emerged in his calculated, strategic approach to his crimes. He meticulously planned abductions and murders, used elaborate ruses to lure victims, and went to great lengths to cover his tracks. The psychopathic aspect of Bundy's personality was clear in his utter lack of empathy, remorse, or concern for his victims. He was able to compartmentalize his crimes and maintain a facade of normalcy in his day-to-day life. Bundy's case illustrates how the Dark Triad traits can combine to create a particularly dangerous and difficult to catch criminal.

The case of Bernie Madoff, perpetrator of one of the largest financial frauds in history, demonstrates how Dark Triad traits can manifest in white-collar crime. Madoff's $64.8 billion Ponzi scheme relied heavily on his narcissistic and Machiavellian qualities. His narcissism fueled an insatiable desire for status and recognition in the financial world. He cultivated an air of exclusivity around his investment firm, making clients feel privileged to invest with him. Madoff's Machiavellianism allowed him to strategically manipulate and deceive on a massive scale. He expertly exploited social connections, used his reputation to disarm skeptics, and crafted an elaborate web of lies to keep his scheme running for decades. While Madoff may not have exhibited the violent tendencies associated with psychopathy, his actions demonstrated a profound lack of empathy and disregard for the devastating impact his crimes would have on thousands of victims. The case highlights how Dark Triad traits can drive individuals to commit large-scale fraud and financial crimes.

Aileen Wuornos presents an intriguing case study of a female serial killer exhibiting Dark Triad traits. Wuornos, who murdered at least seven men in Florida between 1989 and 1990, displayed clear psychopathic tendencies in her lack of remorse and emotional detachment from her crimes. Her difficult upbringing and years of abuse may have contributed to the development of these traits. Wuornos's narcissism manifested in her grandiose self-image as a justified vigilante, claiming her murders were acts of self-defense against violent johns. This narcissistic delusion allowed her to rationalize her actions and maintain a sense of righteousness. Machiavellian traits emerged in her manipulative behaviors, particularly in her relationships with lovers and friends whom she used for money and support. Wuornos's case demonstrates how Dark Triad traits can interact with trauma and societal factors to produce violent criminal behavior in women, challenging stereotypes about female killers.

The infamous Charles Manson provides a compelling example of how Dark Triad traits can be leveraged to manipulate others into committing crimes. Manson's narcissism was evident in his messianic self-image and belief that he was destined for greatness. He cultivated a guru-like persona, convincing followers that he possessed special insight and power. Manson's Machiavellianism allowed him to expertly manipulate vulnerable young people, exploiting their insecurities and desire for belonging to build a devoted cult following. His psychopathic traits enabled him to detach emotionally from the violence he orchestrated, viewing his followers and victims as mere pawns in his grandiose plans.

Manson's case illustrates how individuals with Dark Triad traits can use their qualities to exert extreme influence over others, even to the point of inciting murder.

The case of Jordan Belfort, the "Wolf of Wall Street," showcases how Dark Triad traits can fuel a meteoric rise in the business world, followed by a spectacular downfall. Belfort's narcissism drove his insatiable appetite for wealth, status, and admiration. He reveled in his image as a financial wunderkind and lived an extravagant lifestyle fueled by fraud. Belfort's Machiavellian tendencies were evident in his sophisticated schemes to manipulate stock prices and defraud investors. He created a culture of moral flexibility at his firm, Stratton Oakmont, encouraging unethical behavior among his employees. While Belfort may not have exhibited extreme psychopathic traits, his actions demonstrated a callous disregard for the financial well-being of his victims. His case highlights how Dark Triad traits can contribute to a toxic corporate culture and large-scale financial crimes.

The BTK Killer, Dennis Rader, provides a disturbing example of how an individual with Dark Triad traits can lead a double life as both a respected community member and a serial killer. Rader's narcissism was evident in his desire for recognition and the taunting letters he sent to police and media. He craved attention and took pride in his crimes, even giving himself the moniker "BTK" (Bind, Torture, Kill). Rader's Machiavellianism emerged in his careful planning and execution of murders, as well as his ability to evade capture for decades. His psychopathic traits allowed him to compartmentalize his brutal crimes, maintaining a facade as a family man, church leader, and Boy Scout troop leader. Rader's case illustrates the chilling ability of individuals with Dark Triad traits to seamlessly blend into society while harboring violent, sadistic urges.

The case of Elizabeth Holmes and the Theranos scandal demonstrates how Dark Triad traits can manifest in the world of tech startups and venture capitalism. Holmes's narcissism fueled her vision of herself as a revolutionary innovator, drawing comparisons to Steve Jobs. She cultivated an image of genius and infallibility, refusing to acknowledge the fundamental flaws in Theranos's technology. Holmes's Machiavellian tendencies were evident in her strategic manipulation of investors, board members, and the media. She crafted an elaborate web of lies and half-truths to maintain the illusion of Theranos's success. While Holmes may not have exhibited classic psychopathic traits, her actions showed a marked lack of empathy for the patients whose health was put at risk by Theranos's faulty blood tests. The case highlights how Dark Triad traits can drive individuals to commit massive fraud in pursuit of status and success in the high-stakes world of tech startups.

Chapter 8: Social Media and the Dark Triad

Narcissism in the Digital Age

Narcissism in the Digital Age has become increasingly prevalent with the rise of social media platforms. These online spaces have created an unprecedented environment for individuals to showcase their lives, achievements, and personas to a global audience. The constant connectivity and instant feedback mechanisms inherent in social media have fostered a culture that often rewards and reinforces narcissistic tendencies.

Social media platforms provide users with powerful tools for self-promotion, allowing them to carefully curate their online image. Individuals can selectively share their most flattering photos, highlight their accomplishments, and present an idealized version of themselves to the world. This curated self-presentation can lead to an inflated sense of self-importance and an exaggerated belief in one's own uniqueness or specialness – key characteristics of narcissistic personality traits.

The ability to reach a potentially vast audience through social media feeds into the narcissistic desire for admiration and attention. Users can broadcast their thoughts, opinions, and experiences to hundreds or thousands of followers with just a few clicks. This ease of reaching a large audience can be particularly appealing to narcissistic individuals who crave constant attention and validation from others.

The instant gratification provided by likes, comments, and shares on social media posts serves as a form of external validation that can be highly addictive, especially for those with narcissistic tendencies. Each notification becomes a small dopamine hit, reinforcing the behavior and encouraging users to seek more attention through increasingly provocative or self-aggrandizing content. This cycle of seeking and receiving validation can lead to an unhealthy dependence on external approval for self-worth.

The competitive nature of social media, where users often compare themselves to others based on metrics such as follower counts, likes, or engagement rates, can exacerbate narcissistic behaviors. Individuals may feel pressure to constantly outperform others or maintain an appearance of success and happiness, leading to exaggeration or fabrication of their achievements and experiences. This competition for attention and status can foster a sense of entitlement and a lack of empathy for others – traits commonly associated with narcissism.

The anonymity and distance provided by online interactions can also contribute to the expression of narcissistic behaviors. Without face-to-face contact, it becomes easier for individuals to disregard the feelings and perspectives of others, focusing solely on their own desires and self-promotion. This detachment from real-world consequences can embolden narcissistic individuals to engage in more extreme attention-seeking behaviors or to lash out at those who challenge their inflated self-image.

Social media platforms often reward controversial or polarizing content with increased visibility and engagement. This algorithmic preference can encourage narcissistic individuals to adopt more extreme positions or engage in provocative behavior to gain attention. The resulting controversy and backlash can further feed their need for recognition, even if it comes in the form of negative attention.

The constant exposure to carefully curated highlight reels of others' lives on social media can also contribute to feelings of inadequacy or envy in some users. Narcissistic individuals may respond to these feelings by doubling down on their own self-promotion efforts or by attempting to tear down others to maintain their sense of superiority.

This can create a toxic cycle of comparison and one-upmanship that further reinforces narcissistic tendencies.

The rise of influencer culture on social media has created new avenues for narcissistic individuals to seek fame and adoration. The prospect of gaining a large following and potentially monetizing one's online presence can be particularly appealing to those with grandiose self-views and a desire for admiration. This has led to an increase in performative behaviors and the commodification of personal experiences for the sake of content creation and audience growth.

The pressure to maintain a consistent online persona can also contribute to the development of narcissistic traits. Users may feel compelled to present an unwavering image of success, happiness, or expertise, even when their real-life experiences don't match this portrayal. Over time, this disconnect between online and offline selves can lead to a fragmented sense of identity and an increased reliance on external validation to maintain self-esteem.

Social media platforms often provide metrics and analytics that allow users to track their performance and reach. For narcissistic individuals, these tools can become an obsession, with every fluctuation in follower count or engagement rate being interpreted as a reflection of their worth. This data-driven approach to social interaction can further reinforce the narcissistic tendency to view relationships in terms of their utility rather than their intrinsic value.

The echo chamber effect of social media, where users are often surrounded by like-minded individuals who reinforce their beliefs and behaviors, can amplify narcissistic tendencies. When surrounded by admirers or sycophants, narcissistic individuals may find their inflated self-views constantly reinforced, making it even more difficult for them to recognize or address their problematic behaviors.

The fast-paced nature of social media, with its constant stream of new content and fleeting moments of viral fame, can exacerbate the narcissistic fear of irrelevance. This can drive individuals to engage in increasingly extreme or frequent attention-seeking behaviors in an attempt to remain in the spotlight and maintain their perceived status.

While social media platforms have undoubtedly provided many positive opportunities for connection and self-expression, they have also created an environment that can nurture and amplify narcissistic traits. The combination of easy self-promotion, instant gratification, and a potentially global audience has proven to be a powerful draw for individuals with narcissistic tendencies. As our digital lives become increasingly intertwined with our real-world experiences, it is crucial to recognize and address the potential negative impacts of these platforms on individual and societal mental health.

Understanding the relationship between social media and narcissism is essential for developing strategies to mitigate its harmful effects. This may involve educating users about healthy online behaviors, encouraging platforms to implement features that promote empathy and genuine connection, and fostering a culture that values authenticity over performative self-promotion. By acknowledging the role that social media plays in shaping our perceptions of ourselves and others, we can work towards creating a digital landscape that supports psychological well-being rather than exacerbating narcissistic tendencies.

Online Manipulation:

The digital realm has become a fertile playground for Machiavellian individuals to exercise their manipulative tendencies. The anonymity and distance provided by the internet create an environment where these individuals can employ various tactics to deceive, control, and exploit others. This section delves into the numerous ways Machiavellian personalities manipulate others online, ranging from subtle influence to outright malicious behavior.

One of the most prevalent forms of online manipulation is catfishing, where Machiavellian individuals create fake online personas to deceive others. These fabricated identities are carefully crafted to appeal to specific targets, often exploiting their vulnerabilities or desires. Catfishers may use stolen photos, elaborate backstories, and even voice-altering technology to maintain their deception. Their motivations can vary from financial gain to emotional manipulation or simply the thrill of deception. The consequences for victims can be devastating, leading to emotional trauma, financial losses, and a profound sense of betrayal.

Cyberbullying represents another dark facet of online manipulation employed by Machiavellian individuals. Unlike traditional bullying, cyberbullying can occur 24/7, following victims into the supposed safety of their homes. Machiavellian cyberbullies often use a combination of public humiliation, private harassment, and social exclusion to torment their targets. They may create fake accounts to gang up on victims, spread malicious rumors, or share embarrassing content without consent. The psychological impact of cyberbullying can be severe, leading to anxiety, depression, and in extreme cases, self-harm or suicide.

Social engineering is a sophisticated form of manipulation that Machiavellian individuals employ to gain unauthorized access to information or systems. This technique involves exploiting human psychology rather than technical vulnerabilities. Machiavellian social engineers may pose as authority figures, create false urgency, or appeal to a target's desire to be helpful. They might use phishing emails, pretexting phone calls, or even in-person impersonation to trick individuals into divulging sensitive information or granting access to secure systems. The consequences of successful social engineering attacks can be far-reaching, potentially compromising personal data, financial assets, or even national security.

Gaslighting, a form of psychological manipulation, has found new expression in the digital age. Machiavellian individuals use online platforms to subtly undermine their victims' perception of reality. They may alter or delete online content, deny previous statements, or manipulate shared digital experiences to make their targets doubt their own memories and judgments. This insidious form of manipulation can erode a victim's self-confidence and mental stability over time, making them increasingly dependent on the manipulator for validation and "truth."

The spread of misinformation and disinformation is another tool in the Machiavellian's online arsenal. By creating and disseminating false or misleading information, they can shape public opinion, influence political outcomes, or simply create chaos. These individuals may use bot networks, coordinated inauthentic behavior, or exploit existing echo chambers to amplify their message. The viral nature of social media platforms allows false information to spread rapidly, often outpacing fact-checking efforts. This manipulation of information can have far-reaching consequences, from swaying elections to inciting real-world violence.

Emotional manipulation is a cornerstone of Machiavellian behavior, and online platforms provide new avenues for this tactic. Manipulators may use love bombing, excessive flattery, or manufactured crises to create emotional dependence in their targets. They might exploit the intermittent reinforcement of likes, comments, and messages to keep their victims hooked, alternating between affection and neglect. This emotional rollercoaster can leave victims feeling confused, anxious, and desperately seeking the manipulator's approval.

Blackmail and extortion have found new life in the digital age, with Machiavellian individuals exploiting the vast amounts of personal information shared online. They may gather compromising information through hacking, social engineering, or by building trust over time. Once they have leverage, they use threats of exposure to control their victims, demanding money, favors, or continued compliance. The fear of personal or professional ruin can keep victims trapped in these exploitative relationships for extended periods.

The gamification of social interactions on many platforms provides another avenue for Machiavellian manipulation. By exploiting the reward systems built into social media, these individuals can create addictive patterns of behavior in their targets. They might use intermittent reinforcement, social proof, or artificial scarcity to keep victims engaged and malleable. This manipulation can lead to unhealthy attachments, excessive time spent online, and a distorted sense of self-worth tied to digital metrics.

Machiavellian individuals also exploit the phenomenon of parasocial relationships – one-sided connections where a person feels a deep, personal bond with a media figure. By carefully curating their online presence, these manipulators create the illusion of intimacy and accessibility. They may share seemingly personal details, respond selectively to fans, or create exclusive content to foster a sense of closeness. This false intimacy can be leveraged to influence opinions, extract financial support, or even mobilize followers for malicious purposes.

The manipulation of online communities and forums is another tactic employed by Machiavellian individuals. They may infiltrate groups, gradually gaining trust and influence before steering conversations or actions to serve their own agenda. These manipulators might create multiple accounts to give the illusion of consensus, use sock puppets to attack dissenters, or exploit group dynamics to isolate and discredit opponents. This manipulation can fracture communities, radicalize members, or redirect group resources and attention.

The exploitation of digital vulnerabilities represents a more technical form of online manipulation. Machiavellian individuals with hacking skills may use malware, phishing, or other cyber attacks to gain unauthorized access to devices or accounts. Once they have access, they can monitor communications, steal sensitive information, or even take control of devices. This level of access provides immense power for blackmail, identity theft, or further manipulation.

Online manipulation by Machiavellian individuals is a complex and evolving phenomenon. As technology advances and online interactions become increasingly central to our lives, the potential for manipulation grows. Awareness, critical thinking, and robust online security practices are crucial defenses against these tactics. Understanding the motivations and methods of Machiavellian manipulators is the first step in protecting oneself and others from their destructive influence in the digital realm.

Trolling and Psychopathy

The internet has given rise to a unique form of antisocial behavior known as trolling, characterized by deliberate attempts to provoke, upset, or antagonize others online. This phenomenon has become increasingly prevalent across various social media platforms and online communities. While trolling can take many forms, from relatively harmless pranks to severe harassment, it often shares common traits with psychopathic behavior, particularly in terms of callousness and a lack of empathy for others.

Psychopathy is a personality disorder characterized by a constellation of traits, including shallow emotions, lack of empathy, callousness, and manipulative behavior. These characteristics align closely with the motivations and actions of many online trolls. The anonymity and physical distance provided by the internet create an environment where individuals can engage in harmful behavior without immediate consequences or the need to confront their victims face-to-face. This detachment from real-world social norms and expectations can exacerbate existing psychopathic tendencies or allow individuals to express latent antisocial impulses.

Research has shown that there is a significant correlation between trolling behavior and psychopathic traits. A study conducted by Buckels, Trapnell, and Paulhus

(2014) found that individuals who scored higher on measures of psychopathy were more likely to engage in and enjoy trolling activities. This connection suggests that the same lack of empathy and disregard for others' feelings that characterize psychopathy may drive the motivations behind online trolling.

One of the key features of psychopathy that manifests in trolling behavior is callousness. Psychopaths often display a marked indifference to the suffering of others, and this trait is evident in the actions of many online trolls. Trolls may post inflammatory or offensive content without regard for the emotional impact it may have on their targets. They may also engage in cyberbullying or harassment campaigns, deliberately seeking to cause distress or harm to others for their own amusement or satisfaction.

The lack of empathy associated with psychopathy is another crucial factor in understanding the psychology of trolling. Empathy allows individuals to understand and share the feelings of others, serving as a natural inhibitor for harmful behavior. However, psychopaths and trolls often lack this capacity for emotional connection, enabling them to engage in hurtful actions without experiencing guilt or remorse. This absence of empathy can lead to escalating patterns of abusive behavior, as the troll remains unmoved by the distress they cause to their victims.

The online disinhibition effect, a phenomenon where individuals feel less restrained in their behavior when interacting through digital mediums, may further amplify the expression of psychopathic traits in trolling behavior. This effect can lower inhibitions and reduce the perceived consequences of one's actions, leading individuals to engage in more extreme or antisocial behavior than they would in face-to-face interactions. For those with psychopathic tendencies, this disinhibition can provide an outlet for their darker impulses, free from the social constraints that might typically regulate their behavior in offline settings.

Trolling behavior often involves a degree of manipulation and deceit, which are also hallmarks of psychopathy. Trolls may create false personas, spread misinformation, or engage in gaslighting tactics to confuse and upset their targets. This manipulative behavior mirrors the tendency of psychopaths to exploit others for personal gain or amusement, without regard for the consequences of their actions.

The motivations behind trolling can vary, but they often align with psychopathic traits. Some trolls may be driven by a desire for attention or notoriety, seeking to provoke strong reactions from others to satisfy their need for stimulation or validation. Others may engage in trolling as a form of power play, deriving satisfaction from exerting control over others' emotional states. These motivations reflect the grandiosity and need for dominance often associated with psychopathy.

It is important to note that not all trolls are necessarily psychopaths, and not all individuals with psychopathic traits engage in trolling behavior. However, the overlap between these two phenomena highlights the potential for social media and online platforms to become breeding grounds for antisocial behavior, particularly among those predisposed to such tendencies.

The impact of trolling on victims can be severe and long-lasting. Targets of online harassment may experience anxiety, depression, and a range of other psychological distress symptoms. The callousness displayed by trolls can leave victims feeling isolated and powerless, especially when the abuse is persistent or widespread. This emotional toll underscores the importance of addressing trolling behavior and developing strategies to mitigate its harmful effects.

Efforts to combat trolling often focus on technological solutions, such as improved moderation tools and algorithms to detect and remove abusive content. However, addressing the underlying psychological factors that contribute to trolling behavior is equally important. This may involve developing interventions targeted at individuals with psychopathic traits or implementing educational programs to promote empathy and digital citizenship.

The relationship between trolling and psychopathy also raises questions about the role of social media platforms in shaping and reinforcing antisocial behavior. The design of these platforms, which often prioritize engagement and viral content, may inadvertently reward trolling behavior by giving it increased visibility and attention. This dynamic creates a challenging environment for fostering healthy online interactions and may require a reevaluation of how social media platforms are structured and moderated.

Understanding the connection between trolling and psychopathic traits can inform more effective strategies for addressing online abuse and harassment. By recognizing the underlying psychological factors that drive trolling behavior, researchers, policymakers, and platform developers can work towards creating safer and more empathetic online spaces. This may involve a combination of technological solutions, psychological interventions, and broader cultural shifts in how we approach online interactions and digital citizenship.

As our lives become increasingly intertwined with digital platforms, the need to address the dark side of online behavior becomes more pressing. The intersection of trolling and psychopathy serves as a stark reminder of the potential for technology to amplify harmful human tendencies. By continuing to study and address these issues, we can work towards fostering a more compassionate and responsible digital landscape that mitigates the expression of psychopathic traits and promotes more positive forms of online interaction.

The Dark Triad and Online Culture

The Dark Triad traits of narcissism, Machiavellianism, and psychopathy have found a fertile breeding ground in the realm of online culture. As digital platforms continue to dominate our social interactions, the impact of these personality traits on our virtual landscapes has become increasingly pronounced. This subpoint explores the broader implications of the Dark Triad on digital culture, focusing on the rise of influencers, the proliferation of toxic online communities, and the gradual normalization of certain antisocial behaviors in the digital sphere.

The rise of social media influencers has been one of the most significant developments in online culture over the past decade. These individuals, who have amassed large followings on platforms such as Instagram, YouTube, and TikTok, wield considerable influence over their audiences' opinions, purchasing decisions, and even worldviews.

While not all influencers exhibit Dark Triad traits, the nature of social media fame often rewards and amplifies behaviors associated with narcissism and Machiavellianism. The constant pursuit of likes, comments, and shares can fuel narcissistic tendencies, as influencers seek validation and admiration from their followers. Moreover, the strategic manipulation of content and audience engagement aligns closely with Machiavellian traits, as influencers carefully craft their online personas to maximize their appeal and influence.

The impact of Dark Triad-influenced influencers extends beyond their immediate followers. As these individuals shape trends and set standards for online behavior, they contribute to a broader cultural shift that normalizes self-promotion, strategic self-presentation, and the commodification of personal experiences. This can lead to a distortion of reality for many social media users, who may feel pressure to emulate the carefully curated lives of influencers or struggle with feelings of inadequacy when comparing themselves to these idealized online personas.

Toxic online communities represent another significant manifestation of the Dark Triad's influence on digital culture. These communities, which can range from extremist political groups to cyberbullying networks, often provide a haven for individuals with high levels of Dark Triad traits. The anonymity and distance afforded by online interactions can embolden those with psychopathic tendencies to engage in harmful behaviors without fear of immediate consequences. Machiavellianism finds expression in the strategic manipulation of information and group dynamics within these communities, while narcissism drives the quest for status and recognition among like-minded individuals.

The echo chamber effect of these toxic communities can amplify and reinforce Dark Triad behaviors, creating a self-perpetuating cycle of negativity and antisocial conduct. Members of these groups may experience a sense of belonging and validation for their harmful beliefs or actions, further entrenching their problematic behaviors. The spillover effect of these toxic communities can be observed in the broader online discourse, where aggressive, manipulative, or callous communication styles become increasingly prevalent.

One of the most concerning aspects of the Dark Triad's influence on online culture is the gradual normalization of certain antisocial behaviors. As individuals are repeatedly exposed to manipulative tactics, emotional abuse, and callous disregard for others' well-being, these behaviors can begin to seem commonplace or even acceptable. This normalization process is particularly evident in the realm of online dating and relationships, where ghosting, breadcrumbing, and other manipulative behaviors have become disturbingly common.

The gamification of social interactions on many digital platforms can exacerbate this trend, as users become desensitized to the emotional impact of their online actions. The pursuit of likes, matches, or followers can lead individuals to adopt more calculated and less empathetic approaches to their digital relationships. This shift in social norms can have far-reaching consequences, potentially bleeding into offline interactions and reshaping societal expectations around interpersonal conduct.

The impact of the Dark Triad on online culture is not limited to individual behaviors but extends to the very structure and design of digital platforms. Many social media algorithms are designed to maximize engagement, often by promoting content that elicits strong emotional responses. This can inadvertently favor posts and users that exhibit Dark Triad traits, as their provocative or manipulative content may generate more interactions. The resulting feedback loop can amplify the visibility and influence of individuals with these traits, further shaping the online landscape in their image.

The prevalence of Dark Triad traits in online culture also raises important questions about digital literacy and psychological well-being. As users navigate an increasingly complex and potentially manipulative online environment, the need for critical thinking skills and emotional resilience becomes ever more crucial. Education around recognizing and responding to Dark Triad behaviors in digital contexts may become an essential component of media literacy curricula.

The influence of the Dark Triad on online culture has implications for content moderation and platform governance as well. Social media companies face the challenging task of balancing free expression with the need to curb harmful behaviors associated with Dark Triad traits. Developing effective policies and technologies to identify and mitigate the negative impacts of these traits on digital communities remains an ongoing challenge for platform developers and policymakers alike.

It is important to note that the relationship between the Dark Triad and online culture is not entirely one-sided. While digital platforms can amplify and reward Dark Triad traits, they also provide opportunities for connection, education, and positive social change. Many online communities foster empathy, collaboration, and prosocial behaviors that run counter to Dark Triad tendencies. The challenge lies in creating digital environments that encourage these positive aspects while mitigating the harmful influences of Dark Triad traits.

As we continue to grapple with the broader impact of the Dark Triad on digital culture, it becomes clear that addressing this issue requires a multifaceted approach. This may include developing more sophisticated content moderation systems, promoting digital literacy and psychological awareness, and fostering online communities that prioritize empathy and constructive engagement. By understanding the complex interplay between Dark Triad traits and online behavior, we can work towards creating a healthier, more balanced digital ecosystem that reflects the best aspects of human nature rather than its darker impulses.

Chapter 9: Can the Dark Triad Be Changed?

Psychological Interventions

The question of whether individuals with Dark Triad traits can be rehabilitated or treated through psychological interventions is a complex and controversial one. Psychologists and researchers have long debated the efficacy of various therapeutic approaches in addressing the core characteristics of narcissism, Machiavellianism, and psychopathy. While some experts argue that these traits are deeply ingrained and resistant to change, others maintain that targeted interventions can lead to meaningful improvements in behavior and interpersonal functioning.

One of the primary challenges in treating individuals with Dark Triad traits is their tendency to lack insight into their own behavior and its impact on others. Narcissists, for example, often have an inflated sense of self-importance and may struggle to acknowledge their flaws or the need for change. Machiavellians, with their propensity for manipulation and strategic thinking, may view therapy as an opportunity to gain an advantage rather than a genuine avenue for personal growth. Psychopaths, known for their shallow emotions and lack of empathy, may find it difficult to engage in the emotional work often required in therapeutic settings.

Despite these obstacles, some therapeutic approaches have shown promise in addressing specific aspects of Dark Triad traits. Cognitive-behavioral therapy (CBT) has been used to help individuals with narcissistic tendencies develop more realistic self-perceptions and improve their interpersonal skills. By challenging distorted thought patterns and promoting healthier coping mechanisms, CBT can help narcissists become more aware of their impact on others and develop greater empathy.

For those with Machiavellian traits, therapies that focus on ethical decision-making and prosocial behavior may be beneficial. These interventions aim to help individuals recognize the long-term consequences of their manipulative actions and develop alternative strategies for achieving their goals. By emphasizing the benefits of cooperation and trust-building, therapists can encourage Machiavellians to adopt more socially acceptable behaviors while still acknowledging their strategic thinking abilities.

Addressing psychopathic traits through therapy presents unique challenges due to the emotional deficits associated with this personality type. However, some researchers have explored the use of emotion recognition training and empathy-building exercises to help psychopaths develop a greater understanding of others' feelings. While these interventions may not fundamentally alter the core traits of psychopathy, they may lead to improved social functioning and reduced antisocial behavior.

Mindfulness-based interventions have also shown potential in addressing certain aspects of Dark Triad traits. By promoting self-awareness and emotional regulation, mindfulness practices may help individuals with narcissistic tendencies become more attuned to their own emotions and those of others. For Machiavellians, mindfulness can foster a greater sense of present-moment awareness, potentially reducing the tendency to constantly strategize and manipulate. Even for those with psychopathic traits, mindfulness may help increase impulse control and reduce reactive aggression.

Group therapy approaches have been explored as a means of addressing Dark Triad traits, particularly in forensic settings. These interventions often focus on developing prosocial skills, enhancing empathy, and promoting accountability for one's actions. By providing a structured environment for social interaction and feedback, group therapy can help individuals with Dark Triad traits recognize the impact of their behavior on others and practice more adaptive interpersonal skills.

Psychodynamic therapies, which explore unconscious motivations and early life experiences, may offer insights into the development of Dark Triad traits. By addressing underlying insecurities, attachment issues, and unresolved conflicts, these approaches aim to promote deeper self-understanding and emotional growth. While the effectiveness of psychodynamic therapies for Dark Triad traits remains a subject of debate, some clinicians argue that they can be valuable in addressing the root causes of maladaptive behaviors.

It is important to note that the success of psychological interventions for individuals with Dark Triad traits often depends on their willingness to engage in the therapeutic process. Many people with these traits may only seek help when faced with significant life consequences, such as legal troubles or relationship difficulties. In such cases, motivational interviewing techniques may be employed to help individuals recognize the need for change and commit to the therapeutic process.

Some researchers have explored the potential of pharmacological interventions in conjunction with psychotherapy for addressing Dark Triad traits. While there is no specific medication designed to target these personality characteristics, certain psychotropic drugs may help manage associated symptoms such as impulsivity, aggression, or mood instability. However, the use of medication in this context remains controversial and requires careful consideration of potential risks and benefits.

Early intervention programs targeting youth with Dark Triad tendencies have also been proposed as a potential avenue for prevention and rehabilitation. These programs often focus on developing empathy, emotional intelligence, and prosocial behaviors in children and adolescents who display early signs of narcissism, Machiavellianism, or psychopathy. By intervening at a younger age, when personality traits may be more malleable, these approaches aim to redirect potentially problematic developmental trajectories.

The role of environmental factors in shaping and maintaining Dark Triad traits has led some researchers to advocate for holistic interventions that address not only individual psychology but also social and environmental influences. This may include family therapy, social skills training, and interventions aimed at improving the individual's broader social context. By creating a more supportive and prosocial environment, these approaches seek to reinforce positive behavioral changes and reduce the rewards associated with Dark Triad traits.

While the potential for change in individuals with Dark Triad traits remains a subject of ongoing research and debate, it is clear that addressing these complex personality characteristics requires a multifaceted approach.

Combining evidence-based therapeutic techniques, tailored interventions, and a thorough understanding of the unique challenges posed by each trait may offer the best chance for meaningful change. However, it is essential to maintain realistic expectations and recognize that complete transformation of core personality traits may not always be achievable. Instead, the focus of psychological interventions may often be on managing behaviors, improving interpersonal functioning, and minimizing the negative impact of Dark Triad traits on both the individual and society.

Moral and Ethical Considerations

The question of whether individuals with Dark Triad personalities can or should be reformed is a complex and contentious issue that touches on fundamental aspects of human nature, free will, and societal values. At its core, this ethical dilemma forces us to confront our beliefs about the malleability of personality, the rights of individuals versus the needs of society, and the very nature of morality itself.

One of the primary arguments in favor of attempting to reform Dark Triad individuals is the potential benefit to society. Individuals high in Machiavellianism, narcissism, and psychopathy often engage in behaviors that are harmful to others, ranging from manipulation and exploitation to more severe antisocial acts. By successfully reforming these individuals, we could potentially reduce the amount of harm inflicted on others and create a safer, more harmonious society. This utilitarian perspective suggests that if we have the means to reduce suffering and increase overall well-being, we have a moral obligation to do so.

However, this view raises questions about individual autonomy and the right to self-determination. Dark Triad traits, while often considered maladaptive or antisocial, are still part of an individual's personality. Attempting to fundamentally change someone's personality could be seen as a violation of their personal identity and free will. There's an argument to be made that individuals have the right to be who they are, even if society at large disapproves of their traits or behaviors, as long as they are not breaking laws or directly harming others.

Another consideration is the potential for misuse or abuse of reformation attempts. If we accept that it's ethically permissible to try to change Dark Triad personalities, who decides which personalities need changing? There's a risk that such power could be used oppressively, with dominant groups in society attempting to "reform" those who simply think or behave differently, rather than those who pose a genuine threat. This slippery slope argument suggests that allowing personality reformation could lead to a form of thought policing or enforced conformity.

The question of whether Dark Triad individuals can be reformed is also relevant to this ethical discussion. If attempts at reformation are likely to be unsuccessful, then subjecting individuals to such attempts could be considered unethical, as it would cause distress and potentially violate personal autonomy without achieving the intended positive outcomes. Current research on the treatability of Dark Triad traits is mixed, with some studies suggesting that certain aspects may be amenable to change while others appear more resistant.

There's also the matter of consent to consider. If an individual with Dark Triad traits voluntarily seeks help or agrees to undergo treatment, the ethical concerns are somewhat mitigated. However, in many cases, these individuals may not see their traits as problematic or may actively resist attempts at change. Forcing treatment on unwilling individuals, even if it's believed to be for their own good or the good of society, raises significant ethical red flags.

From a virtue ethics perspective, we might ask whether attempting to change Dark Triad personalities aligns with virtues such as compassion, justice, and respect for human dignity. On one hand, helping individuals to develop more prosocial traits could be seen as an act of compassion, both for the individuals themselves and for those they might otherwise harm. On the other hand, respecting human dignity might require us to accept people as they are, flaws and all.

The potential for unintended consequences must also be considered. Even if we could successfully reduce Dark Triad traits in individuals, we don't fully understand what role these traits might play in their overall psychological functioning or in society at large. Some argue that traits like narcissism, in moderation, can drive ambition and innovation, or that Machiavellian strategic thinking can be valuable in certain leadership roles. By attempting to eliminate these traits entirely, we might inadvertently cause harm or lose potentially valuable contributions to society.

There's also the question of responsibility and culpability. If we accept that Dark Triad traits are largely the result of genetic and environmental factors outside an individual's control, does this reduce their moral responsibility for their actions? And if so, does this strengthen or weaken the case for attempting reformation? Some might argue that if individuals aren't fully responsible for their personality traits, society has a greater obligation to help change them. Others might contend that this lack of responsibility means we should focus on managing behaviors rather than changing fundamental personality traits.

The resource allocation aspect of this dilemma cannot be ignored. Attempts to reform Dark Triad individuals would likely require significant time, effort, and financial resources. There's an ethical question of whether these resources would be better spent elsewhere, such as on education, poverty reduction, or other initiatives that might prevent the development of Dark Triad traits in the first place.

Cultural and contextual factors add another layer of complexity to this ethical dilemma. Different societies may have varying tolerances for Dark Triad traits or different ideas about what constitutes harmful behavior. What one culture sees as a personality in need of reform, another might view as a valuable trait. This raises questions about cultural imperialism and the imposition of one society's values on another.

Legal and human rights considerations also come into play. Depending on the methods used, attempts to change personality traits could potentially infringe on various human rights, such as the right to freedom of thought or the right to refuse medical treatment. Any approach to reforming Dark Triad individuals would need to carefully navigate these legal and ethical boundaries.

Ultimately, the question of whether Dark Triad personalities can and should be reformed does not have a clear, universal answer. It requires us to balance competing ethical principles, weigh potential benefits against risks, and consider the complex interplay between individual rights and societal needs. As our understanding of personality and its malleability continues to evolve, so too will the ethical discourse surrounding this issue. What remains clear is that any approach to dealing with Dark Triad personalities must be grounded in a careful consideration of these ethical implications, respecting both the rights of individuals and the well-being of society as a whole.

Hope for Healing

The question of whether individuals can escape the grip of the Dark Triad traits is complex and multifaceted. While these personality traits are often considered stable and enduring, research suggests that there is room for change and growth. It is essential to recognize that the path to transformation is neither quick nor easy, but with dedication, self-awareness, and professional support, individuals exhibiting Dark Triad traits can make meaningful progress towards more adaptive and prosocial behaviors.

One of the primary challenges in addressing Dark Triad traits lies in the inherent resistance to change often exhibited by those who possess these characteristics.

Narcissists, Machiavellians, and psychopaths may view their traits as advantageous or even superior, making them less likely to seek help or acknowledge the need for personal growth. However, this resistance is not insurmountable. As individuals face the consequences of their actions and experience the negative impact of their behaviors on their relationships and overall life satisfaction, they may become more open to the possibility of change.

Therapeutic interventions play a crucial role in helping individuals with Dark Triad traits develop empathy, emotional regulation, and more positive interpersonal skills. Cognitive-behavioral therapy (CBT) has shown promise in addressing some of the maladaptive thought patterns and behaviors associated with these traits. By challenging distorted beliefs and promoting more balanced thinking, CBT can help individuals develop a more realistic self-image and improve their ability to form genuine connections with others.

Mindfulness-based approaches have also demonstrated potential in mitigating some of the negative aspects of Dark Triad traits. By fostering self-awareness and encouraging individuals to observe their thoughts and emotions without judgment, mindfulness practices can help reduce impulsivity and increase emotional regulation. This increased self-awareness can be particularly beneficial for those with narcissistic tendencies, as it may help them develop a more grounded and authentic sense of self.

For individuals with psychopathic traits, interventions that focus on developing empathy and moral reasoning have shown some success. While the capacity for empathy may be limited in those with high levels of psychopathy, research suggests that with targeted interventions, some improvement in empathic responses and prosocial behavior is possible. These interventions often involve perspective-taking exercises and exposure to scenarios that elicit empathic responses, gradually building the individual's capacity for understanding and relating to others' emotions.

It is important to note that the effectiveness of interventions may vary depending on the severity of the Dark Triad traits and the individual's willingness to engage in the process of change. Those with milder manifestations of these traits may be more amenable to intervention and experience more significant improvements. In contrast, individuals with more severe or entrenched Dark Triad characteristics may face greater challenges in modifying their behaviors and thought patterns.

The role of environmental factors in shaping and maintaining Dark Triad traits cannot be overlooked. While these traits have a genetic component, they are also influenced by upbringing, social experiences, and cultural factors. This underscores the importance of creating environments that discourage the development and expression of Dark Triad traits. By promoting empathy, cooperation, and ethical behavior in families, schools, and communities, we can help reduce the prevalence and impact of these traits in society.

Prevention and early intervention are key strategies in addressing the Dark Triad, particularly among younger generations. By identifying early signs of these traits in children and adolescents, it becomes possible to implement targeted interventions before the traits become deeply ingrained. This may involve teaching emotional intelligence, empathy, and prosocial skills from an early age, as well as addressing any underlying factors that may contribute to the development of Dark Triad traits, such as trauma or attachment issues.

Education plays a vital role in raising awareness about the Dark Triad and its impact on individuals and society. By incorporating information about these traits into school curricula, we can help young people recognize and understand manipulative or exploitative behaviors. This knowledge can empower them to protect themselves from individuals with Dark Triad traits and discourage the development of these characteristics in themselves and their peers.

Media literacy is another crucial aspect of prevention, particularly in the digital age. Teaching young people to critically evaluate the messages they receive through various media channels can help counteract the glorification of Dark Triad traits often seen in popular culture. By encouraging a more nuanced understanding of human behavior and relationships, we can foster a society that values empathy, authenticity, and genuine connection over manipulation and self-interest.

The workplace is another important arena for addressing Dark Triad traits. Organizations can implement policies and practices that discourage the expression of these traits and promote ethical leadership. This may include incorporating character assessments in hiring processes, providing training on emotional intelligence and ethical decision-making, and creating accountability systems that discourage manipulative or exploitative behaviors.

While the path to change for individuals with Dark Triad traits may be challenging, it is not without hope. The plasticity of the human brain and the potential for personal growth throughout life suggest that change is possible, even for those with deeply ingrained patterns of behavior. However, this change requires a multifaceted approach that combines individual effort, professional support, and societal initiatives.

Ultimately, the key to addressing the Dark Triad lies in fostering a culture that values empathy, cooperation, and ethical behavior. By raising awareness about these traits and their impact, we can create a society that is less susceptible to manipulation and exploitation. This involves not only helping those who exhibit Dark Triad traits to change but also empowering others to recognize and resist these behaviors.

The journey towards a society less influenced by Dark Triad traits is ongoing and requires sustained effort from individuals, families, educators, mental health professionals, and policymakers. While complete eradication of these traits may not be realistic, significant progress can be made in mitigating their negative impact and promoting more positive alternatives.

By investing in prevention, early intervention, and ongoing support for those seeking to change, we can create a future where the grip of the Dark Triad is weakened, and the values of empathy, authenticity, and mutual respect prevail. This not only benefits individuals struggling with these traits but also contributes to the creation of a more compassionate and cooperative society for all.

Conclusion

As we conclude this exploration of the Dark Triad, it's important to reflect on the profound influence that narcissism, Machiavellianism, and psychopathy have on individuals, relationships, workplaces, and society at large. Throughout this book, we have delved into the minds of those who exhibit these traits, dissecting their motivations, behaviors, and impacts on the world around them. What has become clear is that the Dark Triad isn't just a theoretical construct—it's a tangible, dangerous force that can leave destruction in its wake. Yet, the understanding of these traits offers an opportunity for awareness, prevention, and even rehabilitation, where possible.

The Dark Triad operates on a spectrum, with individuals exhibiting varying degrees of narcissism, Machiavellianism, and psychopathy. Each trait brings unique characteristics, but when combined, they create a personality that is manipulative, self-serving, and often dangerous. Narcissism, with its focus on self-admiration and entitlement, can lead to an inflated sense of superiority and a lack of empathy. Machiavellianism is characterized by cold, calculated manipulation, where the ends justify the means, regardless of the moral implications. Psychopathy, the most extreme of the three, adds a layer of callousness, impulsivity, and a blatant disregard for the well-being of others.

One of the key takeaways from this book is the realization that these traits are not isolated. Narcissism, Machiavellianism, and psychopathy frequently overlap, reinforcing and amplifying each other. This synergy creates a dangerous psychological profile, capable of causing significant harm in various contexts. Whether in personal relationships, professional environments, or societal roles, individuals with Dark Triad traits are often successful at manipulating, exploiting, and damaging those around them for their own gain.

The implications of the Dark Triad extend beyond the individual level. In Chapter 4, we explored how these traits interplay, not only within the psyche of those who possess them but also in broader societal structures. From the rise of toxic leadership in the workplace to the manipulation of public opinion in politics and media, Dark Triad personalities can rise to positions of influence, often leaving a trail of ethical breaches and societal disillusionment.

This impact is evident in romantic relationships as well. Narcissists may seduce their partners with charm and attention, only to become emotionally abusive when their needs aren't met. Machiavellians are experts at gaslighting and manipulation, often using their partners for personal gain without any real emotional investment. Psychopaths may engage in emotionally or physically violent behaviors, lacking any guilt or remorse. In these cases, the fallout for victims can be profound, leading to emotional trauma, loss of trust, and long-term psychological scars.

In the workplace, the Dark Triad can foster toxic environments where manipulation, backstabbing, and unethical behavior are normalized. Leaders with these traits may rise through the ranks by taking advantage of others, often at the expense of organizational integrity and morale. They tend to create cultures of fear and competition, driving a wedge between colleagues while promoting their own agendas. The consequences are not only detrimental to individual employees but also to the overall health of the organization.

In the context of crime, we explored how Dark Triad traits can manifest in both violent and non-violent forms of criminality. Psychopaths, with their lack of empathy and impulsive nature, are often linked to violent crimes, while Machiavellians might engage in white-collar crimes, leveraging their ability to deceive and manipulate others. Narcissism plays a role in both, as the individual's inflated sense of self-importance may lead them to believe they are above the law.

The digital age has provided fertile ground for the Dark Triad to thrive. Social media, in particular, offers narcissists a platform to seek constant validation, while Machiavellians use the anonymity of the internet to manipulate others behind the scenes. The online world also allows psychopaths to troll, harass, and engage in antisocial behavior with little consequence. This has had a ripple effect on online culture, where toxic behavior is often normalized, and individuals with Dark Triad traits can easily find communities that reinforce and support their destructive tendencies.

The rise of influencers and internet celebrities has further blurred the line between healthy self-promotion and narcissistic exhibitionism. On platforms like Instagram and TikTok, the algorithm rewards those who can capture attention, often pushing individuals with narcissistic traits to the forefront. This digital environment creates a feedback loop, encouraging users to embrace narcissistic tendencies in exchange for likes, shares, and followers.

One of the most important questions we addressed in this book is whether individuals with Dark Triad traits can be changed or rehabilitated. The answer is complex. Psychotherapy and other forms of psychological intervention have shown some success in helping individuals with narcissistic traits become more self-aware and empathetic. However, treating individuals with Machiavellianism or psychopathy has proven more challenging, as these traits are often deeply ingrained and resistant to change.

In many cases, people with Dark Triad traits lack the motivation to change because their behaviors often serve them well in terms of achieving personal gain. Without an internal desire for self-improvement, it is difficult to engage them in meaningful therapeutic work. Moreover, the ethical dilemma of trying to "fix" individuals who may not want to be fixed raises important questions about the role of therapy and personal autonomy.

However, hope remains. Early intervention, particularly in childhood, may be the key to preventing the full development of Dark Triad traits. By fostering environments that promote empathy, emotional intelligence, and ethical decision-making, society can mitigate the impact of these traits before they take root.

As we draw to a close, it is crucial to emphasize the power of awareness in defending against the Dark Triad. Understanding these traits allows us to recognize them in others, and sometimes within ourselves. By being aware of how narcissism, Machiavellianism, and psychopathy manifest, we can make informed choices about who we allow into our lives, how we navigate toxic relationships, and how we protect ourselves in professional settings.

Awareness also extends to a broader societal level. By recognizing Dark Triad behavior in public figures, leaders, and influencers, we can hold individuals accountable for unethical actions and advocate for healthier, more empathetic systems of leadership and social interaction.

The Dark Triad represents a troubling aspect of human nature, one that has the potential to cause widespread harm. But by understanding these traits, their origins, and their impacts, we equip ourselves with the tools to counteract them. This book has aimed to shed light on the twisted minds behind the Dark Triad and to encourage readers to remain vigilant in their interactions, while also fostering empathy, self-awareness, and ethical integrity in their own lives.

In a world where manipulation, deceit, and callousness can sometimes seem to dominate, it is through knowledge and empathy that we find the strength to resist, and ultimately, to thrive.